Acting, Archetype, and Neuroscience

"*How do we move actors into the less accessible regions of themselves and release hotter, more dangerous, and less literal means of approaching a role?*"

In *Acting, Archetype, and Neuroscience* Jane Drake Brody draws upon a lifetime's experience in the theatre alongside the best insights into pedagogical practice in the field, the work of philosophers and writers who have focused on myth and archetype, and the latest insights of neuroscience, to answer this question.

The resulting interdisciplinary, exciting volume works to:

- **Mine** the essentials of accepted acting theory while finding ways to access more primally based human behavior in actors
- **Focus** on the actor's body as the only place where the conflict inherent in drama can be animated
- **Uncover** the mythical bones buried within every piece of dramatic writing, the skeletal framework upon which hangs the language and drama of the play itself
- **Restore** a focus on storytelling that has been lost in the rush to create complex characters with arresting physical and vocal lives.

A radical new mixture of theory and practice by a highly respected teacher of acting, this volume is a must-read for students and performance practitioners alike. It weaves together a wealth of seemingly disparate performance methods, exciting actors to imaginatively and playfully take risks they might otherwise avoid.

Jane Drake Brody is a former Associate Professor in Performance at The Theatre School, DePaul University in Chicago having retired in 2015. Prior to that, she was head of undergraduate acting at Louisiana State University. Jane also founded Jane Brody Casting (now PR casting) in Chicago and Acting Studio Chicago.

Acting, Archetype, and Neuroscience

Superscenes for rehearsal and performance

Jane Drake Brody

Routledge
Taylor & Francis Group

LONDON AND NEW YORK

First published 2017
by Routledge
2 Park Square, Milton Park, Abingdon, Oxon OX14 4RN

and by Routledge
711 Third Avenue, New York, NY 10017

*Routledge is an imprint of the Taylor & Francis Group,
an informa business*

© 2017 Jane Drake Brody

The right of Jane Drake Brody to be identified as author
of this work has been asserted by her in accordance with
sections 77 and 78 of the Copyright, Designs and Patents
Act 1988.

British Library Cataloguing in Publication Data
A catalogue record for this book is available from the
British Library

Library of Congress Cataloguing-in-Publication Data
A catalog record for this book has been reqested

ISBN: 978-1-138-82260-3 (hbk)
ISBN: 978-1-138-82261-0 (pbk)
ISBN: 978-1-315-74247-2 (ebk)

Typeset in Sabon
by Apex CoVantage, LLC

This book is dedicated to my husband, Walter Leo Brody, to the estimable Ben Piggott, and to all of the actors who have helped to make my life such a wonderful journey.

Contents

Figures

Tables

Preface

"O time! thou must untangle this, not I; 'tis too hard a knot for
me to untie!"

Viola, *Twelfth Night,* Act II, scene 2

As I prepare to finish this book, my only thought is "Yes, but there
is so much more." The numerous studies, papers, dissertations,
books, and philosophical writings concerning what it means to be
human and consequently how one best assists an actor to move
from his or her own limited and boundaried life into an imagined
limited and boundaried life could be discussed ad infinitum. My
aim is to synthesize the work of the philosophers, psychological
theorists, anthropologists, scientific researchers, and theatre practitioners whose ideas have inspired me to investigate a way of working grounded in their new thought. I have never been particularly
creative, but I have always been a magpie, able to link unrelated
ideas with each other. I am humble before these and other creators
and know that I can never actually accomplish what it is that I wish
to do. However, I have always lived by the phrase, "Let your reach
exceed your grasp," and so I am reaching to write my thoughts to
spark ideas in others for new means of working.

For my theatre practitioner colleagues, I am too intellectual; for
my academic colleagues, I am too much of a practitioner; and for
my scientific colleagues, I am too ignorant of science. For these
reasons, I think that I am the perfect person, with the kindness of
others, to join together seemingly separate disciplines into a coher-
ent praxis for actors and directors.

In writing a book, one always needs to ask oneself, "For whom
is this written?" My answer is simply people like myself: Teachers,

directors, actors, and other citizens of the theatre who desire to get to the bottom of things. I will try to speak clearly in jargon-free language, to translate science where needed, and to provide as many examples as the length of this book can tolerate. My mission is not to overwhelm anyone with my erudition; I simply want to draw some dots from mythology to biology to acting and back again. My work is an attempt to connect the primal sources of emotion to unregulated actions and thence to the creation of archetypes (or gods) that when externalized have, since prehistory, both regulated and safely accounted for these passions. Once this is realized, my belief is that the language of the text so drenched in chemistry and sweat will burn into the bodies and souls of both actors and audiences.

The list of brilliant acting theoreticians, directors, and pedagogues is immense. Before I begin I would like to give my respect, gratitude, and admiration to those who had a direct effect on my thinking, in no particular order:

Jacques LeCoq
Wendell Beavers
Ann Bogart
Tyrone Guthrie
Declan Donnellan
Dr Paul Kassel
Dr John Schranz
Charles Marowitz
Peter Brooke
Miss Mary Virginia Rodigan
Mike Alfreds
Konstantin Stanislavski
Michael Shurtleff
Dr Frank Whiting
Dr John Kirk

I would also like to acknowledge the enormous help of my volunteer assistant editor, Jacob C. Stanton; my husband, Walter L. Brody; my sister, Patricia Haberlein; Jeremy Pfaff; and the rest of the actors who agreed to be videoed doing *In the Blood* Superscenes: Leea Ayers, Christian Cook, James Bernard Gilbert, Lenora Hayden, Charles Johnson, Christopher Jones, Jeri Marshall, and Jessica Maynard. Thanks are also due to Dustin Whitehead for putting the video together so beautifully.

Introduction

Konstantin Stanislavski, the father of acting pedagogy, who lived 1863–1938 in Moscow, Russia, was a teacher, actor, and director who applied a systematic approach to discovering the best way for actors to work. His final work was called the *Method (or System) of Physical Actions* or psychophysical action.[1] It focused on the physical underpinnings of action and the uses of improvisation. While his texts consider action to be both activity such as moving a chair and interaction with another such as pleading for mercy, my feeling is that, prior to his death, Stanislavski was heading toward a definition of action removed from mundane activities like chair moving.

Action for him was at its most valuable when it was directed at another person, i.e., second person interactivity. The idea of second person interactivity will be discussed later in the book. He called such action "living through the part" or "living the part," or 'experiencing.'[2]

In 2012, John Gillett, the noted British actor, teacher, and Stanislavski scholar, in *Stanislavski Studies*, Vol. 1, attempts to describe the idea of "experiencing," which was Stanislavski's translator's best way of expressing the original Russian word *perezhivanie*.

When I *experience*, as opposed to telling myself consciously what I should be doing, I have a number of qualities. I am focused and easy, absorbed and engaged in the imaginary circumstances of the improvisation or script, in the action, in the predicament of the character, as if the situation is real, so that I believe this is happening in the sense of imagining with commitment it's happening: I make believe with naivety like a child. This is when I start to feel I am (or as Benedetti puts it more actively, I am being) this character in this moment, in this situation, here and now. *I go through the action moment by moment focusing only on the actor/characters opposite me and what's happening to me and them, trying to affect and change them with what I want, as I would interact with people in real life.* This experience of the action and interaction with other people is the basis of the actor's art for Stanislavski: 'Acting is action – mental and physical' (*An Actor's Work*: 40). He conceives this to occur as a spontaneous, flexible, and free process within the given structure of the circumstances and the discipline of the practice of an art.

(p. 87; author's emphasis)

Among other things, Gillett illuminates a key concept in acting that is frequently missed and usually undervalued in the pursuit of character definition and emotion by actors and directors. In life, we do what we do, and we are who we are, because we interact with one another on a psychophysical level. We change each other chemically as we confront other beings in our world. Humans are more verbs than nouns; they are never at rest for long. We are created to function in a society.

American actors and their teachers have for the past eighty years focused on either felt emotion or on creating a role from an imaginary template of attributes and attitudes without the far more important element of action and interaction in the relationships. Action in this way is looked at as residing in the plot.

The idea that we feel what we feel, behave the way we behave, and do what we do because of our history and our expectations of the people around us is given insofar as action is concerned. Either of these methods – self-generated emotion or the belief that identity is static – results in a product that unwittingly postulates that we are separate and self-created. Science, philosophy, and psychiatry have been telling us that this is not true for almost a century. Yet actors continue to either lacerate themselves to achieve self-created feelings or falsely demonstrate who the character 'is' for the audience and the approval of the director.

I am equally opposed both to the method of emotional manipulation and to the concept of character creation. Both approaches are begun in the intellect and usually remain there. Neither excites the audience because both can lead to the actor's worst sin – in-going self-consciousness. An actor trying to generate feelings is like an anorexic whose liver is consumed as he or she tries to attain the unhealthy bodily fantasy. The character-driven actor who presents a semblance of what he thinks he is supposed to be ends up judging the character and eliminating the most fascinating part of human nature, its inconsistency.

In most instances for actors/directors/pedagogues, the focus has been 'character' as an unchanging feeling unit, without the concomitant element of action. Or the character may change for good and all at the end of the play never having shown any likelihood of alteration until the line, "Oh, now I see, I will be brave and true from now on." The concept of character as a delimited object, judged either intellectually or sentimentally by the director or actor with no regard for the actions and relationships that actually delineate character, is wrongheaded. I had a discussion the other day with an actress who reported that the director had told her that her character was "just a snob." If this had been a sit-com she was working on, I might have let it go, but it was a very good play written by George Bernard Shaw, and I decided that the project was probably not going to be successful.

Reading a play several times and then deciding who this "guy" or "gal" is restricts discovery and experimentation from the very beginning of the process. What is it the actor or director is actually seeing? My contention is that the images that arise have more to do with the psychological limits of the reader than they do with a solid foundation upon which to mount the play. The actress who has been told that she is "just a snob" has been told to stop working and do a stereotype. Her director's reductiveness is also present with actors who, when questioned, generally describe their "character" in derogatory and dismissive ways, as in "he's a real jerk!" or "she is just a bimbo." They reveal a special glee when making these statements. Perhaps their joy comes from saying things that they know are suspect. How are we to reveal the play's main argument if so many of the people in it are so lacking in complex human qualities? How are we to have a healthy society if this kind of laziness is honored? Such simplistic thinking leads to the sort of government and society that is intolerable for most of us.

I have heard many actors say, "Hey, the bad guy doesn't think he is bad," which is good as it goes, but this is usually followed up with the statement, "So, I just have to play him like a good guy!" My answer is that the idea of good guys or bad guys has no place in a director's or an actor's vocabulary. It is vital, especially in this time of religious and political extremism, that we force the *audience* to judge the rightness or wrongness of a situation or a person on their own. The theatre must present the problem, whether comically or tragically, and the audience must decide what to do about it. It begins with the actor and the director.

I realize that this flies in the face of Brecht and socially or politically conscious theatre making, but I maintain that both forms can reduce humans to stereotypes that, in the end, defeat their very purposes. Propaganda is always a lie. If a character does despicable actions, the actor is responsible for making these plausible and understandable, not for making it easy for the audience to judge and walk happily away. Brilliant actor Michael Shannon, when responding to an interviewer assertion that his character was a "jerk," responded by saying (I am shortening this), "I don't think so. I think he's lonely and that he needs to sell houses." The actor's job is to be the best defense attorney for his or her actions; let the audience prosecute. There is an old phrase that can help in this. "There, but for the grace of God, go I." Because we are all human, we are therefore all capable of any action if driven far enough. The actor and director must find out what the stakes are that drive the action before they set out to condemn it or the doer.

I think that the reason for all of this confusion is primarily misreading and underreading poorly translated books by Stanislavski or books attributed to him that he in fact did not write, along with the erroneous conflation of his work with that of the American teacher Lee Strasberg. Strasberg taught acting using an in-going Freudian psychological approach, and as an inveterate publicity seeker, he allowed people to believe that his teaching was what Stanislavski intended. After some conflicts with Stella Adler and Bobby Lewis, who had actually visited with Stanislavski and brought back a clear map of his system, Strasberg said that he was not doing Stanislavski, but his own method. This map is included in the addendum at the end of this book. It was originally published in Robert Lewis' book, Method or Madness, New York, Samuel French, 1958.

In reality, Stanislavski had discarded the psychological approach many years before Strasberg ever began teaching. For reasons of history and technology, Strasberg's approach, which is admittedly useful for film but not stage, became the predominant form of training in the U.S. This situation finally led to the recent fashion to ignore both Strasberg and Stanislavski, even though most people have neither read nor studied either of them.

I believe that Stanislavski had it right within the given circumstances of his own life. We, as theatre artists in the twenty-first century, must examine his work and build on that which is helpful and reject that which is no longer useful. It may make more sense now to do some basic research in philosophy, psychology, neuroscience, and biology as a means of testing his hypotheses.

I deeply admire the ideas of philosopher and anthropologist Ernest Becker, whose Pulitzer Prize winning book, *The Denial of Death*, concerning human personality construction as an out-going and active element of life makes sense to me. Another school of psychology/philosophy/sociology of great help for actors and directors is Symbolic Interactionism, which posits that we are complex beings, never finished, always in the process of becoming. It suggests that there is no central, stable self; rather, we are made up of many opposing elements, each of which has it uses. Carl Gustav Jung (C.G. Jung), a student of Freud's who rejected most of his theories, gives us a symbolic view of life with his belief that we are born with preexisting responses to archetypes and symbols to assist in our development and identity creation.

It is true that we can never fully know nor understand ourselves or others, and trying to do so is a party game because, in the end, we are all mysteries. All we can do to discover who any of us "are," if that word is even applicable, is to observe our behavior. That behavior is perceived through what we *do*.

Among these theorists I take my stand concerning the irrelevance of the pursuit of "who is this person" and say that "what must I do" is the more important investigation. If behavior is a result of emotion converted into action, our questions must be "what is the action and what prompts it?" As we are all biologically mammals, the base of our lives is survival and the need to flourish, both a primitive and modern need.

My intention is to remarry text with the primal intention/action/emotion underlying it. The underpinnings of the text are therefore not a translation of the text; rather, the text can be seen to emerge through emotional conflicts in the relationships that give rise to language as a compromise to avoid overt action. These interactions are the components of what we call "character."

Notes

1 Dewey, John. Essay. *Nature, Life and Body-Mind*, 1928. While Stanislavski probably had not read Dewey, it is interesting that they both coined the phrase, Stanislavski in Russia and Dewey in the U.S. They

were both referring to the idea of Body-Mind, or Bodymind, as it were. Jean Benedetti. *Stanislavski and the Actor.* New York: Routledge/Theatre Arts Books, 1998; Sonia Moore. *Stanislavski Revealed: The Actor's Guide to Spontaneity on Stage.* New York: Applause Theatre Books, 1991.

2 Stanislavski, Konstantin. *The Actor's Work.* trans. Jean Benedetti. New York: Routledge/Theatre Arts Books, 1998.

Part 1

Origins

Chapter 1

Returning to mythic roots

Ever since there have been actors, directors, and playwrights, theatre practitioners have attempted to discover the secret formula by which to deeply affect an audience. The wrangling among the proponents of external techniques (voice, posture, and language skills) with advocates of intense inner work for the actor (psychology and emotion) has been never ending and generally circular. An actor attempting to be vocally and physically adept will inevitably be psychologically and emotionally affected. The actor who favors the pursuit of emotion and psychology as his or her means of creating a character will inevitably be physically affected. Even with the over fifty-year explorations by the greatest theoretician of them all, Konstantin Stanislavski, nothing definitive has been found. The nearest we have come is the postulation by him that in order to affect an audience in an emotional way, the actors within the play must themselves be personally involved.

He implied that the audience could somehow distinguish between actual thought/emotion and technically facile presentation. This idea, in turn, lead to a search by theatre artists for how to best accomplish this feat. Since Stanislavski's appearance on the world stage, artists such as Sanford Meisner, Tadashi Suzuki, Lee Strasberg, Uta Hagen, Peter Brook, Jerzy Grotowski, Anne Bogart, Declan Donnellan, and thousands of other directors, actors, and theoreticians have experimented, using everything from extreme and exhausting physicality, primal scream, intensive psychotherapy, prescribed movements, and vocal explorations beyond simple vocal production. All have contributed to an advanced stage of actor training with a plethora of approaches, each of which is partially effective, and each of which speaks to different actors differently.

Regardless of the approach used, at the core of all acting theory, whether Stanislavski-based or not, is the need to tell a story that affects an audience. The narrative needn't be linear or fully spelled out, but it must exist. Whether the actor is deeply involved psychologically or not, in order for the story to be recognizable to an audience, actors must do actions that lead to comprehensible outcomes. If the actor is personally and psychologically involved, if intentions are clear, the storytelling will be more meaningful because it attracts the audience on a deeper level. *An action in this case is defined as something one character does to another character to achieve a desired end; such actions, while physically based, are expressed both physically and verbally.* While I realize that many theoreticians use a much broader idea of action, my feeling is that in the final analysis it is the actions between and among people that are of true dramatic significance. It is only through others that we can succeed on any quest.

Physical beginnings of acting

In prehistory, at the beginning of theatre, playing, joking, physical jousting, miming, copying others, showing off, sexy dancing, and tricks were all probably part of the show. The tribal fireside must have elicited serious and playful reenactment of hunting stories, sad retellings of lost loved ones, and horrific recountings of mysterious natural disasters, as well as funny send-ups of known community figures. While there are many theories concerning the whys and wherefores of myth, the celebration/ritual was a way to avoid danger, to assuage the nature gods, to heal a sick member of the tribe, and to unite it for the betterment of all. As the original stories became favorites of the tribe, the forces of nature were given names and faces, heroes became demigods, and all were connected to families of their own. These magical stories became ritualized, codified, edited, and repeatable.

Even now, children left alone to play create dramas with little or no regard for realism, as naturally as they eat and sleep; making theatre appears to be an integral part of our learning and socialization. They also tend to criticize others who "don't do it right," or the "way we did it before," or "according to the rule," which implies an agreed-upon narrative with boundaries and expectations. I prefer to be an acting teacher who doesn't mind the bossy kids and who wishes to reawaken the sense of play and inventiveness that is natural to us all.

We appear to be hard wired for spirituality, which in turn appears to be linked to our attempts to make art. We stand in awe of power and size, and the source of the artistic search seems to be related to an attempt to understand the mysteries of an alien world both internal and external. Creating gods and religions as a means of communicating and understanding the universe is a hallmark of most human civilizations. Most societies have a creation story with a Mother and/or Father Earth, a Mother and/or Father of the Sea or of the Sky or the Mountain or other natural features that are relevant to the culture. Birth, sex, death, and resurrection are universal themes. The immortal powers procreate as needed either amongst themselves or with humans to supply a family of gods, demons, demigods and heroes that represent essential human needs, interests, fears, joys, and vices. These beings differ from humans and are not held to standards of human morality. They do whatever they wish and use humans as their playthings.

Myths, the early stories of these "super beings," became a dominant part of the aesthetic, intellectual, and religio-spiritual life of the community. As historical communities were conquered or merged with others, the local heroes and gods were often drafted into the religion of the conquerors. At times they were added to an existing god who had similar qualities, e.g. Venus and Aphrodite, or they may have been adopted fully if such a god hadn't been a part of the conqueror's hierarchy. These stories emphasized the magical connections to heroes, gods, demigods, half-remembered ancestors, protectors, and persecutors to their worshipers.

While theorists differ as to which came first, the myth or the ritual, once these stories transformed into performance, the legend carriers – shamans, priests, and griots – took possession of their delivery and were charged with keeping the secrets and ceremonies for their fellows. They were expected to be conveyors of powerful narrative essences for the sake of the group, even though the stories might change some of the immaterial facts by accident or for effect. These "myth-men," as Kenneth Burke[1] labeled them, were connected to the spiritual ideas of their village or town. It is only human nature that these chosen individuals would make themselves necessary to their societies as mysterious and special creatures speaking in fanciful terms and creating new, more exciting narratives.

Whether or not the poets of the enchanting and mysterious past were charlatans, magical shamans, or something very like, they were either born into their profession and trained by their parents or were chosen as a result of some oddity of temperament or physical constitution to capture the spirits of the community to which they belonged. They needed to be connected somehow to the ineffable, accessible only through ritual and dream states.

As communities were conquered, disintegrated, folded into others, or simply moved, it is likely that the legend carriers were forced to perform for strangers as well as their tribal relations. Many would have had to move from being semi-stable members of a fixed community to "professional" figures supported by the more powerful members of the society. As this transition occurred, I speculate that the spiritual or religious aspect of the actor/shaman's job became less important as the need to entertain overwhelmed the formerly priestly duties. The sacred duty to protect and guide the souls of the community became the province of the priesthood, and the former holy clowns were released from that responsibility.

We know that by the time of the Greeks, even though they were still connected in a minor way to the gods, players were considered to be outside of polite society and generally needed to move from place to place to make a living. It was undoubtedly necessary for these player/bards to develop great vocal, physical, emotional, and intellectual talents in order to keep food on the table. With only their voices and their bodies, they kept the myths, heroes, and history of the people concerned alive, changing names and places where necessary.

Once playwrights emerged, actors became mouthpieces for the dramatist. Their fate may have been a bit better as a result of the new popularity of the theatre, but few were able to lead lives of comfort or stability. Their employers were governments, royalty, wealthy individuals, and the church.

After the fall of the Roman Empire, we know both male and female actors, minstrels, mimes, bards, troubadours, and others in Western civilization returned to their original duties as creators of their own texts. While it is not proven, my belief is that the commedia dell'arte evolved from Roman comedies and became a means of making a living during the Dark Ages. The form does not depend on playwrights or knowledge of a particular language or culture; it uses stereotypes and stories found in Greek and Roman comedy and requires only a few actors, some props, some masks, maybe a wagon, and a performance space. The commedia players relied first on movement, dance, song, and gestures to excite their audiences – in effect, a return to the tribal campfire.

As the Renaissance slowly progressed across Europe and Great Britain, actors once again became the deliverers of the playwright's words and thoughts. They were generally attached to companies of other actors often composed of families and maintained their own repertoire. We know that these players retained a certain improvisational style and a great deal of audience interaction within the new theatrical forms and that their performances featured singing, dancing, and physical clowning.

It is not my purpose to deliver the history of acting in this book. My aim is to contrast the traditional apprentice/family/group way in which actors were trained with the more formal situation of training today. In our civilization, actors are rarely raised by shamanist parents, nor are they children of vagabond players. They are not expected to write their own material, nor are they forced to please the king. They frequently attempt to form companies, but the economics of today's world make such an endeavor almost impossible. Now, people who wish to become working actors usually substitute professional training for the formerly maturational ways in which the skill was acquired. People who feel the call to perform and who render themselves up to professional training still hear the spiritual call of Dionysius, but in our practical-minded world, the voice is easily ignored.

Current actor training

> *"Art is that which is recognizable to the soul."*
>
> James Joyce

As a young woman, it was my privilege to witness some of the greatest theatre of the twentieth century. These brilliant works included Peter Brook's *A Midsummer Night's Dream*, *The Dragon Trilogy* by Robert LePage, *The Revenger's Tragedy* at the Royal Academy in London, *The Cherry Orchard* directed by Mike Alfreds, *A Search for Signs of Intelligence in the Universe* by Jane Wagner performed by Lili Tomlin, and *Hang Onto Your Head* in Minneapolis performed by the Children's Theatre Ensemble and directed by John Donahue. Luckily, a year ago, I had the same experience watching *The Glass Menagerie* at the Mary-Arrchie Theatre in Chicago directed by Hans Fleishmann. These performances still live in my mind as collective spiritual experiences that lifted the entire audience as a mass into realms of joy and suffering combined. The performances shook us, picked us up, and turned us around in our seats. When such a wonder is witnessed, it binds us to our fellow audience members. In *Midsummer's*, we literally stood on our seats for twenty minutes screaming as the cast tossed paper plates into the house and we lofted them back. Lily Tomlin's solo performance had the sophisticated New York audience weeping and laughing with awe, pity, and pride in the courage of humans. All of these offerings had three things in common: they were metaphoric, highly physical, and nonrealistically true. The same can be said for the recent phenomenon "Hamilton" currently on Broadway. My search to spark such greatness in my students stems from these encounters with the divine theatre.

At present, actor training, in the U.S. at any rate, has become an industry; and those of us in it seem to be at a moral and ethical crossroads. On the one hand, we want to prepare actors of depth and skill for an artistic life, however poverty-stricken, in the theatre that we know can move mountains. On the other hand, we feel morally bound to ensure that our students are ready for the more economically rewarding demands of media.

Given the current state of the profession, how can we once again touch the magic of the shamanistic performer? How can we elicit actors of power and beauty? I believe that it is necessary to find a method to once again open actors to a quality of playing that is theatrical in size as well as truth, regardless of genre. We must prepare them to create hundreds of more "Hamilton"s.

At the present time acting classes that privilege "realism" are the dominant mode of teaching, partially because actors with such skills are able to move into commercials and television easily. And, as television is the way most students first understand acting, everyone is mollified. This idea of realism has convinced a generation of actors that realism is actually truthful and that anything other than a "kitchen sink" approach to performance is somehow not real/true.

Several years ago, I directed a production of the Charles Mee play *Big Love* as a final project for the freshman acting class at the university where I worked. The show is nonrealistic, loud, silly, and lots of fun. After the curtain came down, a fellow acting teacher approached me to say that she had enjoyed the goings-on but was unable to decide if the students in it could act. Her paradigm for actors did not include much beyond television. Her definition of acting had been narrowed to include only performances of small size and intimacy. While most of us would agree that such moment-to-moment work is perfect for many things and must be taught, it doesn't mean that audience interaction and illogical happenings are outside of the purview of theatre and acting.

For many such people, including directors, actors, and teachers, if a playwright doesn't use contemporary means of expression, if the story has little to do with sociology or psychology, it is viewed as "style" and therefore not true. If the staging or the dialogue veer from the contemporary concept of realistic, it is viewed as a "style" piece and therefore not real. The prosaic belief that realism is true is not questioned. As I see it, "realism" has come to mean something to do with a material, predictable, and describable world; it includes easily comprehensible non-lyrical language and quotidian behavior from the actors, often employing a small emotional range and rarely including physical or vocal extremities. It is safe.

This "realism" in all likelihood has to do with the specific requirements of film and television. Screenwriters are encouraged to eliminate as much dialogue as possible, the theory being that the best film is the most silent and the story needs to be told visually. The best films don't talk much. On television, writers of series and sitcoms must write within very specific time and budget limitations as well as work within the contractual constraints of the stars of these vehicles. There are many other rules and restrictions placed on both screen and television writers, and thus a style is born. Because most of us watch television or films on a daily basis, this style of writing and acting appears to be realism. It is no more realistic than the so-called reality shows that have been so popular over the last decade.

As a result, today's actors, reared on television and film, have difficulty finding truth in plays that use anything more than the laconic speech and movement patterns typical of the mediums. They are fearful of committing the biggest sin of all, being "over the top." They avoid extremities of any kind. Plays written in the far past, as well as those written only thirty years ago, are often suspected of not being "real" because they don't look or sound like the media. I believe that we must encourage actors and other theatre makers to recognize that "realism" is as much a style as Shakespearean acting or Greek messenger speeches and choral work. Extremes of any kind are the foundation of theatre, and when such passions are rejected, the theatre collapses in on itself.

So, what is style, anyway? Strictly speaking, it is a way of looking at life based on predominant cultural values and doing things based on those values in a particular time and place. For instance, the overt romanticism of the black and white films made during the World War II era was a reflection of an approach to life that the society in question found meaningful and "realistic." Young people watching these movies today find them "over the top" and are often amused at the overt emotionalism. The author Clifford Odets, a member of the Group Theatre, wrote plays such as *Awake and Sing* that were considered searingly real in their time. Now, dramas with characters who speak at length using metaphor and poetic overtones, or who speak using the slang of the period, seem overly melodramatic or simply funny to many young actors. John Osborne's *Look Back in Anger* feels as if it is from another universe for the under-40 crowd. None of these plays were considered "style" plays in their time, and none of them are any less true today despite their forgotten realism. How will hip-hop theatre look to the people of the future? Surely they will wonder if such behavior is a common viewpoint and parlance for many of us.

There is only one verifiable truth. We die. Other than that, it is all speculative. From my point of view, truth is a thing that is only available through image and metaphor; we cannot accurately describe our own truth because it is not tangible. The truth of the lives of humans is not inscribed by what many would call reality; we are much larger than we may wish to admit. Truth has nothing to do with the calendar or with the passage of time. Our dream lives, our struggles to make sense of an absurd world, are anything but obvious and may seem illogical to the casual observer. These are the things of which theatre is constructed. The other is soap opera or sociology or psychology and hasn't enough spiritual or emotional impact to last for more than an afternoon. Truth sticks around for centuries and haunts us. I often think when I go to the theatre that if there is a sofa and a cocktail table on the stage, we need to be careful. Of course, magnificent shows such as *A Delicate Balance* or *August Osage County* have sofas and tables and chairs, but the plays themselves are more like bad dreams than realistic slices of life. We somehow recognize and reverberate with the characters in them whether or not we have experienced anything like the situations they present. If well done, these works force us to be aware of the plight and courage of individuals being tested in a chaotic world. There are no answers contained in them, only mysteries.

Current training

Of course, in the U.S. most acting training programs devote a certain amount of time to the classics, or more specifically to Shakespeare, whose plays are by their nature nonrealistic. The teachers of such courses have a two-fold job. First they must convince their students that Shakespeare is worth doing, even though it is HARD, and second, they must fulfill their contractual obligation to distinguish the Bard from other playwrights. The emphasis is often put on rhetoric, literary beauty, scansion, and vocal skills. Rightly so; that is what heightened language requires. But student actors trying to please the overloaded teacher produce dry and unwatchable work. Generally the instructor has little inclination or time to work with the primal actions and passions underlying Shakespeare that gave rise to the poetry in the first place.

It can also happen that many American instructors of Shakespeare eschew these technicalities in an attempt to seduce student actors into believing that "these folks are just like us!" (In the USA, those indulging in fancy talk and behavior are looked on suspiciously.) Such an approach makes the students feel good, but in reality this dumbed down approach is not good practice for anyone. It may be acceptable for non-actors or high school students, but for professionals this method usually results in greatly diminished productions. Many years ago, I attended a production of *Hamlet* at a regional theatre in New York. The actor doing the lead was an excellent though mannered film actor who had begun his career in the theatre. He seemed to have been converted to some odd form of realism through ignorance! He chose to have a character from the play on stage to receive his soliloquys. I suspect this absurdity had to do with his fear of breaking the fourth wall, as most Shakespeare demands. The actor, who shall be nameless, got the following review in the *New York Times*, which indicted the director for the ridiculous choices. (I suspect that the director was greatly influenced by the movie star under his aegis.)

> Hamlet tosses off "Get thee to a nunnery" as an aside, slaps Ophelia across the face and then a few moments later, out of sequence, delivers "To be or not to be" as a direct address to the lady. He embraces her on the word "contumely," before he gives her a bare bodkin.[2]

Of course, I have also seen a modern version of *Hamlet* at a well-respected theatre conservatory wherein the 'To be or not to be' speech was projected from a cellphone as a twitter '2brn2b' and Claudius was having a torrid affair with Ophelia. I am fairly certain that this was an attempt at making *Hamlet* more sexy and relevant to a college audience. Both productions of the play seem to be afraid to grapple with Shakespeare's genius. I wonder if any of the actors or directors involved had ever witnessed brilliant and completely understandable Shakespeare such as The English Theatre Company's rendition of the history plays with Michael Pennington.

Movement and voice classes continue to move in exciting realms of experimentation and expansion for the actor's instrument. However, such work is far removed from the students' acting classes, where small moment-to-moment acting is the aim. These teachers are often frustrated by a lack of time and a feeling that somehow they are not valued. As TV and screen actors do not seem to need it as much, the voice and bodywork on the actor's instrument is often given lip service. I have to admit that, years ago, I was extremely worried that a voice teacher assigned to coach my production and do dialect training would make the actors self-conscious. This excellent teacher was not a member of the everyday rehearsal team and came into rehearsals only three times toward the end of the process. My fears were not without merit, but her expertise moved the actors ahead without any damage. I learned to respect her art form and wished that she had been at every rehearsal. Time and money usually preclude such a luxury.

Because of this structure, in all but the richest of theatres, Descartes rules the day: the mind and body are separate! As in my own experiences, the synthesis between acting and voice/movement is usually limited to choreography or choral work or to specific movement difficulties and vocal clarity, the idea being that these "technical" problems should be addressed outside of rehearsal in private sessions with the voice or movement teacher, even though these teachers can tell you that most difficulties stem from timidity and fear on the part of the "realistic" actor. If while in rehearsal or performance the actor is thinking about his/her voice, or posture, or gesture, literal self-consciousness will ensue. It must be the job of the director and voice and movement specialists to find organic reasons to marry all aspects of a performance as a team.

I once heard a renowned voice teacher say to a young woman doing a classical monologue where she was addressing a royal figure, "Is that the way YOU would greet the present Queen Elizabeth if you were to meet her at court? Show me how you would do THAT." The adjustment both vocally and physically was immediate and centered in the relationship to royalty. It was a wonderful acting lesson. The actor had never taken training in courtly behavior, but her own understanding of status created a credible scene. When she was shown how to curtsy and stand by the movement specialist, she loved learning how to do so. Her knowledge functioned as an aid to her behavior just as it would a real subject of the crown. Furthermore, she could be good at it, and that is always gratifying!

The idea of theatricalism – the very word 'theatrical' – has been debased by many actors and directors. Educational theatre, as well as a large proportion of professional theatre, appears to have discarded the excitement, the danger, and the wonder involved in witnessing actors of courage conquering the physical, spiritual, and emotional mountaintops that arrest audiences by their audacity. Who would tell Peter Brook that his *Midsummer Night's Dream* was too theatrical? How would the actor Danny Davis (later famous for the sitcom, *The Butler*) be allowed to pull down a 50- by 50-foot curtain of red silk, roll himself in it, pull a lover off of her seat into the red cocoon, make love to her and burst forth angrily in a production of *The Misanthrope* at The Tyrone Guthrie Theatre (as occurred in a performance directed by Garland Wright in 1987)? I don't think that Mr. Davis complained that his character "wouldn't do that."

At present, the most exciting theatres in the world, theatres like the Pantheatre, Theatre du Soleil, Siti Company, Lookinglass, et al, are attempting to reclaim this magical theatre – one that is explosive, nonlinear, physical, and visceral. This movement owes its life to Peter Brook, Yevgeny Vakhtangov, Judith Malina and Julian Beck, Jerry Grotowski, Bertolt Brecht, Antonin Artaud, Vsevolod Meyerhold, Ann Bogart, Mary Overlie, Jean LeCoq, Tadashi Suzuki, and other visionaries for whom live theatre had to be (a) live and unpredictable for its audiences. However, in their fervor, many of the companies doing such work neglect playwrights, text, and verbal ability in favor of directorial cleverness, spectacle, and acrobatic skill. They borrow much from musical theatre without acknowledging their debt.

Although the works of these forward-looking companies are frequently beautiful and admirable, textual meaning is easily neglected or lost entirely. The danger presented by this stimulating work is that it can dismiss or downplay narrative and linear textual argument. This is a vexing civic problem when it comes to more sophisticated discourse and rhetoric in a society currently addicted to random noise and image overload.

It goes without saying that the audience for musicals is far larger than for any other form of theatre. Why is this true? I believe that the draw is their "nonreality." Musicals are theatrical: They don't pretend to mirror everyday life; they put forth story and fantasy. They make no pretense to being real, and yet they are able to emotionally move the spectators with ease. It may be that the "right-brained" concept is at play in that music has the ability to transcend logic and rational thought into an emotional space more easily than any other art form.

The "straight" theatre was at one time able to stir its audiences with power and delight. However, with the advent of new media, predominantly television, and the absolute belief in "realism" as the arbiter of truth, the nonmusical theatre has withered on the vine. With few exceptions, the only straight plays that sell well across the country are those featuring movie stars. The storefront movement, which is gathering momentum, is exciting, but those who work in it are poverty stricken, and the audiences tend to be limited to "those in the know." They are not on the radar of the person in the street. There are exceptions popping up in the regional theatres, but their audiences are limited, and these same adventurous theatres must seasonally prop up their funding with *The Christmas Carol*, pantomimes, and well-known musicals.

Many large and well-endowed institutional theatres rely on known writers and dramatic literature, with an emphasis on spectacle. The artistic staffs of these venues desire to give their patrons exciting new works, but these scripts usually must be measured against the audience's willingness to see something they have never heard of before. Of course, there are a few great regional theatres who have trained their patrons to come through careful marketing, and planning, but these are in the minority. These theatres speak well, move well, and make a profit. The audiences leave the productions smiling but rarely realizing the thunderous power of theatre. I am aware that I am generalizing concerning our institutional theatres; however, I have witnessed far too many performances where the "emperor had no clothes on."

In the U.S., currently there are several television series that capture the sort of pure theatricality that energizes an audience. They include *Breaking Bad*, *Game of Thrones*, *Orange is the New Black*, *Empire*, and *House of Cards*. In each, the archetypal characters function from such primal needs that we watch transfixed not only at their triumphs but also their tragic falls. The enormous popularity of these shows points to the audience's desire to be in the presence of heroes and mythical stories.

As an example, Walter White in *Breaking Bad* can be seen as an Oedipal figure, cursed with cancer and evil from the beginning of the series. His relationship with his disabled son, Walter White Jr., is distant, while his connection to his 'adopted' son, Jesse Pinkman, is deep and passionate. Walter's story has to do with masculinity defined partly as someone capable of overt physical action and dominance with little regard for the "feminine" virtues.

In looking at myth, there are many doors that lead in the same direction and many variations on the ancient stories. In this case, Walter White Sr. can certainly be likened to the god Hephaestus, the god of fire, the son of Zeus and Hera, the blacksmith of the gods, and an alchemist, who controlled fire to create splendid furniture and weapons by turning ore into shining objects. He was given a magnificent workshop by the gods and created robots to do his work in it. He was crippled and had two sons who were also lame. Hephaestus was rejected by the other gods not only because of his affliction but because he gave his skill with fire to mortals. This gift deeply offended the Olympians, but he was forgiven sometime later and allowed back into paradise.

Hymn: To Vulcan (Hephaistos), fumigation from frankincense and manna

> Strong, mighty Vulcan (Hephaistos), bearing splendid light,
> Unweary'd fire, with flaming torrents bright:
> Strong-handed, deathless, and of art divine,
> Pure element, a portion of the world is thine:
> All-taming artist, all-diffusive pow'r,
> 'Tis thine supreme, all substance to devour:
> Æther, Sun, Moon, and Stars, light pure and clear,
> For these thy lucid parts to men appear.
> To thee, all dwellings, cities, tribes belong,
> Diffus'd thro' mortal bodies bright and strong.

> Hear, blessed power, to holy rites incline,
> And all propitious on the incense shine:
> Suppress the rage of fires unweary'd frame,
> And still preserve our nature's vital flame.
>
> From the *Hymns of Orpheus*,
> translation by Thomas Taylor[3]

When first seen, the two sons of Walter White Sr. are Walter White Jr. and, metaphorically, Jesse Pinkman. Walter White Jr. is a sweet, kind, loving, loyal, and obedient child with no capacity for physical strength or cruelty. He is crippled and dependent on others, the very thing that most frightens his father. Walt Sr. does not consciously see himself as rejecting Junior, but in actuality he does. In ancient times, Junior would have been exposed on a hilltop at the command of his father. The impulsive, quicksilver Jesse, on the other hand, is a drug addict, also a disability, but it is not physically apparent. He is opposite to Junior in his approach to the world. The pure theatricality of *Breaking Bad* with its fearful villains and extreme situations is similar to video games featuring heroes and villains, blood and battles. However, it acknowledges the complexity of life while yet retaining its horrific primal behavior.

Video games like *Call of Duty* or *Gears of War* do not generally consider the complexity of character that *Breaking Bad* and its ilk do, but they also emerge from myth recycled into new journeys, both dark and dangerous, for young people to experience. Added to that list must go the more palatable and enduring popularity of the *Harry Potter* books as well as *The Lord of the Rings* saga.

Summation

Is it possible that the live theatre can no longer compete with the impact of such artistic uses of the media? If we are to have any relevance at all, I believe that we must develop ways to create actors capable of achieving the sort of mythic and spiritual truth that attracts viewers to the best video games, television, and film can offer. We must ensure that the physicality of our performances, whether expressed or repressed, is more tangible than our TV brethren. We must free ourselves from the privileging of small moment-to-moment psychologically based realism better suited to the screen. We must focus instead on regaining the ability to excite audiences and actors through the power of theatre to move audiences spiritually and emotionally. We must embrace our original role of myth-men and magicians who draw crowds through play and mystery.

Notes

1 Coupe, Lawrence. *Kenneth Burke on Myth: An Introduction*. London: Taylor and Francis Press, 2005.
2 Gussow, Mel. "Hamlet with Walken in Connecticut." *New York Times*, August 23, 1982.
3 *The Hymns of Orpheus*, trans. Thomas Taylor (1792). Philadelphia: University of Pennsylvania Press, 1999 (current edition). Retrieved from http://www.theoi.com/Text/OrphicHymns2.html#65.

Chapter 2

Resurrecting
mythic stories

This book is titled *Acting, Archetype, and Neuroscience* because of my belief in the power of mythic stories and archetypes to resurrect lost and forgotten dreams in both actors and audiences. Such reconnections to the ancient spiritual and shamanist roots of acting can produce work of depth and physical beauty. Neuroscience is leading the way in discovering the nature of action and the visceral effects of witnessing it on observers. For audiences, a mythic focus can link a community back to itself through the recognition of shared humanity regardless of the historical or sociological setting of the drama. It is thanks to Joseph Campbell and his towering work, *The Hero with a Thousand Faces*, that I have come to seek the deeper reality of a story and not its cultural trappings.

I was first introduced to the work of the mythologist and writer Joseph Campbell when he burst onto the public scene in 1968 with the *Power of Myth* interview series. Owing to the inspiring conversations between Bill Moyers and Mr. Campbell, many artists were influenced to revisit myth and archetype as a font of artistic creation. Campbell's emphasis on the shared journey of all lives, the Hero's Journey, has changed the way in which many of us view life and art. Among the artists who acknowledge a debt to Campbell are George Lucas (*Star Wars*), Christopher Vogler (*The Lion King*), composer John Cage, the Wachowski family (*The Matrix*), folksinger and poet Bob Dylan, novelist Richard Matheson (*I Am Legend*), choreographer Martha Graham, and many others.

Ernest Becker, mentioned earlier, won the Pulitzer Prize five years later in 1973 for his book *The Denial of Death*.[1] In it he theorizes that what motivates humans most is the fear of death, in contrast to Freud's assertion that sexual adjustment is the essential force behind human behavior. Becker asserted that in trying to overcome our inevitable demise, we try to snatch a level of immortality, by creating what he terms a "hero project": "Man cannot endure his own littleness unless he can translate it into meaningfulness on the largest possible level."[2] We do so by aligning with a power greater than ourselves that will live on past our miserably short historical existence. We ensure this semi-eternal status through having children, joining religions, fighting in wars, building businesses, making art, gaining political, social, or financial power, or even becoming die-hard fans of sports teams. These things give us an identity as well as the certain knowledge that we belong to something special. As Luisa, the girl in the musical *The Fantasticks*, says, "Please God, please, don't let me be normal." In a sense, we attempt to become demigods, heroes, angels, and even demons so long as we have a sense of being a part of life beyond personal death. Becker acknowledges our dual nature:

> Man is out of nature and hopelessly in it; he is dual, up in the stars and yet housed in a heart-pumping, breath-gasping body that once belonged to a fish and still carries the gill-marks to prove it. His body is a material fleshy casing that is alien to him in many ways – the strangest and most repugnant way being that it aches and bleeds and will decay and die. Man is literally split in two: he has an awareness of his own splendid uniqueness in that he sticks out of nature with a towering majesty, and yet he goes back into the ground a few feet in order blindly and dumbly to rot and disappear forever.[3]

While Becker's writing is not exactly fun to read, he hits on verities that we cannot deny. Joseph Campbell uses this sense of futility to describe the rationale behind man's search for meaning in myth and gods. He gives us a direct link to the idea of the "hero's project."

Campbell himself owes a debt to James Joyce as well as writers and philosophers such as Thomas Mann, Joseph Spengler and Jiddu Krishnamurti. Becker likewise utilized the writing and thought of Otto Rank, Arthur Schopenhauer, and Soren Kierkegaard. Both Becker and Campbell based much of their work on C.G. Jung's exploration of archetype and were in agreement concerning Jung's postulation, "an image can be considered archetypal when it can be shown to exist in the records of human history, in identical form and with the same meaning."[4]

Campbell's thinking on art can be encapsulated in the following quote used in several of his books. James Joyce, in his novel, *A Portrait of the Artist as a Young Man,*[5] "True art must arrest the viewer in its presence and fill him with both pity and awe as it unites the viewer with 'the secret cause.' " For Campbell, this was the highest definition of art. An example of this in present day is the response by visitors to the Vietnam Wall in Washington DC. One needn't have lived through that war, nor lost anyone in it, to be arrested and filled with pity by its simple grandeur.

The mythologist and anthropologist Mircea Eliade[6] refers to art as "that which allows the audience/viewer to enter *sacred* time and space for a glimpse of a power that is sensed but not seen." He connects art to ritual as a means of transporting a community and its individuals through trials of difficult social and political transitions that might otherwise tear the society apart. Certainly, the theatre at its center is a ritual that aims to bring people together to share a problematic experience from which they will emerge changed in some way. The transition is implied.

When these great thinkers are viewed together, the journey of the hero and the journey of humans, regardless of cultural trappings, become clear – the journey of the hero reflects *internal* and *spiritual* travel through an *external* interaction with the world. A recent film made from the novel of the same name, *The Life of Pi*, can be experienced in just this way. Outwardly the story is about a man trapped on a boat in the ocean with a vicious tiger; inwardly it is about the courage to survive, the mystery of existence, and the necessity of faith.

I am, of course, aware that the idea of universality suggested by these concepts has been denigrated in academic circles over the past fifty years or so. Nevertheless, as an acting teacher, director, casting director, obsessive reader, and researcher, I believe that great acting takes place when the actor releases the protection of his/her personality construct and surrenders judgmentally to the basic biological human possibilities in all of us, both for good or ill.

Archetypes defined

Archetypes are emanations of our biology; Jung described them thusly: "Our instincts (archetypes) are biological fact."[7] Images of the archetypes and gods are always waiting in our developing mind. We must find a practice to connect the actor biologically with the awe-inspiring and magical in life embedded in our unconsciousness. It is our biological response to the world that is universal, not sociological values or cultural concepts.

There is much ongoing debate concerning how to understand archetypes: Are they the platonic "first ideal forms" preexisting real forms i.e. the "ideal first chair" versus the real chair? The idea of a preexistent perfection is something held by culture over eons. The need and search for preexisting gods is a prime example. How does this differ from a stereotype or a prototype?

I believe that the difference is that, like us, archetypes are dual, part angel/part demon, or as Becker would have it, part worm. An archetypal figure is double natured; it contains two elements, one of construction and the other of destruction. Each of those elements can split again and again, like an atom. Insofar as archetypal heroes go, this is what distinguishes Aphrodite from the iconic though stereotypical Marilyn Monroe. Aphrodite is the epitome of female sexuality; however, because of her divided nature she is perfectly capable of destroying anyone who crosses her. She is not feminine. Marilyn Monroe has been likened to such goddesses. However, her oddly childlike sort of soft sexuality did not admit of the revenge and mayhem that also attaches to Aphrodite. If she had used such strengths, she might be alive today.

Linking neuroscience and archetypal mythology

Over the past fifteen years, the advances in neuroscience, as a result of the functional Magnetic Resonance Imaging machine (fMRI) has allowed scientists to see almost directly into the workings of the brain through electronic computer-created images. The fMRI makes it possible to see neurons as hot spots that "fire" as they light up when activated (see Figure 2.1. Courtesy of Refik Kanjhan of the School of Biomedical Sciences, the University of Queensland, Australia).

This all happens beneath our consciousness and prior to a conscious recognition of their activation. In the case of *motor* neurons, which are responsible for grasping and other forms of primary movement, our *desire* for a big juicy apple is registered, and the appropriate neurons begin arranging for our hand to reach for an apple before we are actually aware of it. The "need to do" precedes the "act of doing" because our emotional brain translates the desire for a taste of the fruit chemically. If we had to think of every physical step along the way, we might never grab an apple. The brain's activity can be seen as *active intention.*

Figure 2.1 Neuron

My first interest in neuroscience began several years ago when I read about a discovery concerning the presence of a type of *neuron* in the motor neuronal areas of the human brain called a mirror neuron. These are motor neurons that are responsible for muscular activity. The discovery was that these motor neurons fire not only when we do something ourselves *but also when we observe an action being done by another*; hence the word "mirror." This statement resonated for me because for many years it had been my working hypothesis that an action was something done to another human, to achieve a desired end. I had also wondered frequently about my own response to actors as I watched literally thousands of scenes as an acting teacher and director. Why did I feel them in my body? Why was I able to pinpoint for an actor what he or she had been feeling or thinking at any given moment? I originally attributed this ability to a skill I developed in watching my rather unpredictable father for signs of impending violence. I still suspect that this is true. I believe that I developed mirror neurons to a high degree to recognize slight shifts in his musculature and be ready to deal with action and conflict.

The Mirror Neuron (MN) Theory has some detractors, but when it comes down to it, the real dispute is with claims made by some scientists that mirror neuronal activity can be generalized out from coordinating muscular movements, to being responsible for empathy and emotional responses. While I am not at all certain that the idea is wrong, I am not actually using that sense of their function.

Another criticism that is somewhat strange is the idea that MN theorists attribute all action to MNs; however, this claim is misleading. The following quote refuting this accusation is from Vittorio Gallese, one of the world's major researchers in MNs.

> In conclusion, it is fair to say that action understanding, even at a basic level, does not necessarily require the activation of MNs. It has been shown that communicative actions, when implying motor acts outside of the human motor competence (e.g., observing a barking dog) are easily understood without any involvement of the observer's cortical motor system (Buccino et al., 2004). However, this does not imply that action understanding obtained without mirroring is the same as that based upon it. I submit that it is only through the activation of MNs that we can grasp the *meaning of others' behavior from within*. In virtue of the translation of others' bodily movements into something that the observer is able to grasp as being part of a given motor act accomplished with a given motor intention, the observer is immediately tuned in with the witnessed motor behavior of others. This enables the observer to understand others' motor goals and motor intentions in terms of her/his own motor goals and motor intentions.[8]
>
> Vittorio Gallese

Importantly for actors and directors, the discovery that motor neurons fire in the observer's muscle/motor neurons in virtually the same neuronal areas as the person whose muscles are actually doing the action leads us to understand that action, reaction, and intention are at the bottom of the audience's attention. This implies that the audience members read intention before action because their brains are reading the unconscious electro-chemical neuronal signals of the doer. In other words, when my desire to reach and grab an apple is first noticed by my own electro/chemical neuronal apparatus, it begins firing. The "firing" happens in the same way and in the same brain location in the observer of my grab for the apple. It is therefore *intention to act* that is read by the audience, *whether the action is fulfilled or not.* (It is also vital to understand that watching a human do something is quite different from watching a dog barking.) Another way of seeing this is in a soccer or football game. The players must be so tuned into the actions of others that they simply respond rather than stopping to consider what might be happening on the field.

At the time that I encountered this startling idea, I was reading *An Actor's Work*, the new translation and compilation by the late Jean Benedetti of Konstantin Stanislavski's writing, wherein Stanislavski says:

> Haven't you ever been aware, in life or onstage, when in communication with other people, of a current emanating from your will flowing through your eyes, your fingertips, your skin? What shall we call this method of communication? Emitting and receiving rays, signals? Radiating out and radiating in? In the absence of an alternative terminology let us stick with these words since they illustrate very clearly the kind of communication I have to talk to you about. In the near future, when this invisible current has been studied by science, a more appropriate terminology will be established.[9]

I was struck by Stanislavski's perception and his belief that science would one day confirm his observations. I am aware that this mystery is still being investigated and that teachers in Russia have developed an almost eerie method by which their students send rays between themselves and cause action in each other such as an unspoken command to "go to the door." For me, mirror neurons are the "rays" or "signals radiating out and radiating in." It seems to me not unusual that a passionate acting pedagogue such as Stanislavski, whose job it was to watch actors succeed and fail for years on end, should intuit what science would later prove. This synchronicity prompted me to look deeper into the field of mirror neurons and to branch out to other neuro-scientific areas of experimentation.

For many performance teachers, these discoveries seem to reflect what we have known all along. We have been creating exercises, etudes, scenes, and improvs to assist in memory, attention, and action in a corporeal way. We knew that talking wasn't at the center of human behavior. Stanislavski was constantly looking to science as well as metaphysics to explain human behavior, Michael Chekhov was fascinated by the link between physical gesture and psychological needs, Jerzy Grotowski was fascinated by questions of "spirit" as well as the power of image and its relationship to the audience and the body, Sanford Meisner revealed the complicated dance of attention to partner in his work, and Bertolt Brecht investigated the actor's capacity to move the audience intellectually through stereotypical images. However, either because theatre is ritual or because audiences naturally create a narrative, the great poet wound up moving them emotionally despite his best attempts.

Neuroscience is telling us that humans are far less self-aware and far more impulsively reactive than we have told ourselves we are. It appears that when we are sensorily influenced by something in our environment that disrupts our internal balance either virtually or literally, and whether pleasantly or not, we experience a chemical warning that things are not as they should be. In the case of the apple, hunger or desire for comfort proves to be the imbalance. This response is the experience of emotion, and its purpose is to incite us to action.[10] We experience emotion to regain psycho/physiological balance through action; it is not an end in itself. It is action rather than emotion that is at the root of both drama and life itself. Archetypes are externalized representations of emotion and action. While this is not a new idea, it is being proven by the new research in brain science. Perhaps a better understanding of our active biology is perhaps a stronger way of igniting both the actor and the audience.

Current neuroscience and learning theory also support the Jungian idea that our brains use three common ingredients of drama – metaphor, generalized archetype, and narrative – as the basis of our ability to both learn and to feel safe in the world as children. We move through the world using images and symbols that open out to other images to make meaning. Image or archetype is compressed meaning.

As neuroscience progresses, we find more and more that there is a great deal of hardwiring in our primal brains having to do with unconscious reactions to the world. We have wiring that allows us to recognize faces as something important, even before the first glimpse of our mother. We are wired to acquire language, find sexual partners who have certain qualities desirable for procreation, and we naturally work in groups and seem to have a need for status and hierarchy within them. The old idea that, unlike animals, people aren't born with instincts has been tossed out. We are animals ourselves, and if we weren't born with a good deal of software, we might never survive. Such software makes us able to hook into specific aspects of the world and its creatures even when we are not aware of doing so. For me, this software is the progenitor of archetypes.

While we may differ dependent on the vagaries of birth and time, we are all the same biologically under the personality constructs we erect to cope with the specific difficulties of our individual, personal lives. Mythic stories address these fundamental similarities, and the heroes and archetypes involved in them represent the urges, energies, and needs that we all share. They are the representations of both the reptilian and the primal brain which make up the system. The reptilian, which is located just above the brain stem, is responsible for breathing, digestion, heartbeat, balance, and learning of movement. It is an unalterable part of the "hard drive" that keeps us alive. Attached to it, just above the brain stem, is the emotional center – for our purposes, the amygdala and the hippocampus – that links the rational with the irrational. This system beneath our consciousness can be said to control almost everything we do, feel, and learn. It is the seat of memory, emotion, planning, and therefore of action itself. There are various names for and interpretations of the contents of the limbic system; however, its functions are not disputed. These two parts of the brain take up only one-third of its volume, and yet they are the source of most of the information stored in the large cerebral cortex.

Summation

Owing to the predominance of the nonintellectual portion of the brain and the need for humans to understand the chaotic world, there is little reason to doubt that the essential stories of humankind emerge not from our rational mind but from the memories and life-saving functions of the "back brain." Even if one were to purposely sit down to write a story, a seemingly intellectual activity, the first hint of creativity would come drifting out of the primal brain to be shaped and handled by the frontal lobes. The story's life beat is behind the ears. In a sense, our brains exhibit the same conflict between order and chaos that is at the bottom of every story and conflict.

Notes

1 Becker, Joseph. *The Denial of Death*. New York: Free Press, Simon and Schuster, 1973.
2 Ibid.

3 Ibid.
4 Jung, Carl. *The Collected Works of C.G. Jung*, trans. R.F.C. Hull. Bollingen Series XX, Princeton, NJ: Princeton University Press, 1960.
5 Joyce, James. *A Portrait of the Artist as a Young Man*. New York: Random House, 1952.
6 Eliade, Mircea. *Myth and Reality*. New York: Harper and Row, 1963.
7 Walker, Steven F. *Jung and the Jungians on Myth: An Introduction*. London: Routledge, 2002.
8 Gernsbacher, M.A., Heyes, C., Hickok, G., and Iacoboni, M. (2011). Mirror Neuron Forum. *Perspectives on Psychological Science* 6 (4), 369–407. D.o.i. 10.1177/1745691611413392.
9 Stanislavski, Konstantin. *An Actor's Work*, trans. Jean Benedetti. London: Routledge Press, 2007, 246.
10 Dewey, John. (Jan 1895). The Theory of Emotion. *Psychological Review* 2 (1), 13–32.

Chapter 3

Primary conflict and the Hero's Journey

There are a finite number of stories and essential relationships in dramas that emerge from our biology, our familial histories, and our dream lives. The narratives are peopled with heroes, gods, and demons; their components are the recognizable tropes of life and as such can be seen as archetypal. They represent the working out of conflicts between and among ourselves, our communities, our nations, our homes, and our gods. The problem of order versus chaos is at the bottom of them all, and we are fascinated by the dichotomy. We are always aware of our duality and the conflict that is an undeniable component of separateness poised against a desire for balance. This need for balance is addressed by Robert McKee, the master screenwriting teacher, whose book, *Story*, is a must read for every actor, director, writer, and citizen of the theatre.

> Story begins when an event, either by human decision or accident in the universe, radically upsets the balance of forces in the protagonist's life, arousing in that character the need to restore the balance of life.[1]

There are those who hold the idea that plays and stories are about good and evil, a simple response to this dynamic. But who is to say if good is based in order or if good is based in chaos? Certainly a society thrives when there is a certain amount of order; without it neither our traffic nor our water would flow. The basic human needs of food, water, and habitat are threatened. We can't express ourselves, we can't grow, if we are worrying about simply getting by. However, too much order restricts the ability of a society to move ahead and prosper. A certain amount of chaos is necessary for growth and exploration to exist. How would we find new rivers, new ways of building, or new food to eat without the freedom to test, the freedom to challenge and to go against the status quo? One might say that the concept of order vs. chaos is the same as the conflict between government vs. freedom. Our political parties are always debating this same issue in differing guises. Should guns be regulated or should they be available to all? Should motorcyclists be forced to wear helmets? Should oil exploration take place in Alaska? It is always the same question, "How much is too much?" The entire problem of living together in society is this eternal conflict on the micro and on the macro level. In order for this never-ending and necessary imbalance to be visited by the audience, each character in the play must embody some position on the scale of order or chaos. In other words, scenes, plays, and narratives are forever about the question of order versus chaos despite their outward manifestations.

The need for balance

In order for a drama to exist, it must be centered in conflict. Within this construction, the characters are tested and either prevail or not; order wins or chaos does; and a moment of balance is achieved. Actors and directors both are generally aware of need for conflict. *What is often missed is the idea that the plot only serves to ignite the fundamental underlying conflict indivisible from all human relationships.* The desire for wholeness and balance, to be fully comprehended by another, is a mainspring of our search for well-being, security, and identity. Until we become angels or Christ-like beings, we cannot perfectly know nor unconditionally love each other; there is always an element of separation, and therefore all of our associations are conflicted by their very nature. In this context, conflict does not mean war or fighting, it means constant renegotiation of relationships, an eternal seesaw, forever trying to achieve the impossible balance of personal, social, political, and spiritual life that eludes us. Within a play, a situation may be ameliorated; the problem between the two characters in it, however, will not change, nor will either change their essential viewpoints. Indiana Jones does not become Woody Allen, but they may find a way to coexist for a while.

The resolution of a dramatic conflict is a result of maneuverings within the relationships of the characters involved; this holds true regardless of genre. The plot serves as a battle ground for these skirmishes to occur. So, too, in myth, dynamic relationships between and among the gods and humans are needed to tell a story.

As humans we are incapable of thinking of behavior beyond our own human propensities. The gods and heroes we have created are simply enlarged crystallizations, and extrapolation outwards, of our own urges to power, comfort, and self-actualization. I have borrowed some phrases of James Hillman, the founder of depth psychology, to express this idea, and paraphrased a portion as well.

The power of myth, the stories of the gods, exists in its magical power to seize and influence psychic life through the use of the ingredients of dreams and primal urges. . . . "The Greeks knew this so well. . . . Therefore . . . psychology shows myths in modern dress and myths show our depth psychology in ancient dress."[2]

Depth Psychology, which owes a great debt to Jungian theory and Ernest Becker, suggests that the characters of myth are anointed with their god-like statuses as a way of handling the fears and possibilities of our own powers. In effect, we divorce and worship the things that we wish to be but feel too small or fearful to accomplish. The hero or god allows us to not only escape the responsibility for our own extreme desires but also to witness its triumphs and punishments. While our modern world seems to lack heroes and gods, we have substituted movie stars, political figures, and sports heroes for them, as well as such intangible and symbolic accomplishments as patriotism, careerism, and financial success.

We refer to the stories of the gods as "myths." These are similar to the first unfiltered way in which as infants we attempt to make sense of the world. The enormous gods, our parents or caregivers, have complete control of our lives. Their behavior has no apparent rationale, and we create stories for ourselves to predict their behavior. Once this narrative is complete, we can begin to predict when we are fed or diapered or entertained. The family ties are then widened to include the early social understandings of people outside of our intimate circles. These are the earliest memories etched in our consciousness and serve as the prototype for all other relationships. Each has its concomitant predictable conflicts and expectations, centered in power and love. In like manner early tribes and later civilizations created myths and heroes to gain a sense of meaning from the seemingly random acts of the gods.

Primary conflict: Order versus chaos

> *"Invention, it must be humbly admitted, does not consist in creating out of void but out of chaos."*
>
> Mary Shelley

Plays have as their skeletons a mix of the essential relationships and stories that in the past have been explicated in myth and ritual. They constitute memories begun in forgotten times and in dreams enacted around campfires. When the actor or director or designer digs deeply to find the bones of these narratives under the layers formed by the accretions of time and place, to reveal these bones bleached and bare, their mythical and archetypal natures are released, and form a bridge for the viewer to the essential meanings obscured by day-to-day life. Both actor and audience are bound together in the time that is "Once upon a time."

Theatre from this perspective can constitute some of the most compelling rituals remaining in our society. It is as if, in re-enacting the primal myth beneath the plot, the actors awaken a set of mirror neurons that remove the separateness of the audience and join it with the actors and with itself. For such ritual re-enactments to take place, powerful and archetypal characters and relationships must be called to the place of battle and engagement.

As I have discussed, while every script is unique and every interpretation is singular, there are no new stories being written, no new types of humans being built (at least not yet), no new human relationships being discovered, and no new emotions bubbling up from the human psyche. Plays and screenplays are all created from the same basic ingredients – *conflict revealed within human relationships that are exploded by plots.* Kenneth Burke the philosopher calls myth "the temporizing of essence,"[3] which is a difficult way of saying that myths are eternal stories that express the fundamentals (essence) of human life regardless of historical time (temporal).

It is owing to this that there are, and must be, archetypal patterns of scenes, predictable patterns of relationships within scenes, patterns of dramatic conflict, patterns of character behavior, patterns of plots, and many others. As discussed earlier, the basic pattern of conflict in human relationships and therefore in dramas and screenplays is the ancient tension between order and chaos. Order is the need in humanity to find security and safety; chaos is the need in society to explore and to grow: The desire to protect versus the desire to explore, the desire for peace vs. the desire for freedom. This need for balance is found on a cellular level in our bodies and in every form of organization from family to government to civilizations. The tug of war is between order that wants to stabilize and open boundaries versus chaos which wants to maximize and expand. Without a certain amount of chaos in the world, nothing new can occur; without order in the world, nothing can grow. Each needs the other and yet each is in constant conflict with the other.

Stories are about the day when one of these is out of proportion to the other. Here are a few examples of this dichotomy in various constructs.

Polka versus jazz

The Beer Barrel Polka or any polka for that matter emphasizes a 4/4 beat, unchanging from the beginning of the music until the end. This musical form is comfortable and upbeat, meant for dancing and celebration. Its songs are short and the lyrics predictable. The songs are the same now as they were when I heard them in a dance hall when I was 4 years old. Polka is modest in its aims and encourages community and continuity.

Dave Brubeck's *Take Five*, on the other hand, changes rhythms and switches keys freely; it incorporates long, ragged, and repeated lyrical lines with uneven and bent notes always present. Jazz is a sophisticated form requiring listening and discernment. It focuses on the skill of the performers even when done by a full ensemble. Jazz is an expression of individualism, deconstructionism, and restlessness.

Static art styles

Piet Mondrian, in the composition pictured in Figure 3.1, reduced color, scale, size, and relationship to a lively series of mere blocks. He used red, yellow, blue, and white. The placement of the color

Figure 3.1 Piet Mondrian, *Composition with Red, Yellow, and Blue*, 1927

Courtesy of the Mondrian Trust.

blocks are precise and strictly boundaried by sharp black lines. He works in exactitude and order.

Picasso, on the other hand, who was also exploring geometric means of deconstructing the world, his cubist period, is here seen working in the same colors and in the same year in Figure 3.2. He has also attempted to reduce the figure to its essential angles. However, he experiences the world through his own lens, which is anything but orderly; the elements of chaos and whimsy in his work come shining through. Notice the little curlicue at the bottom right of the picture.[4]

Figure 3.2 Pablo Picasso, *Femme dans un Fauteuil*, 1927

©2015 Estate of Pablo Picasso/Artists Rights Society (ARS), New York.

Peter and Wendy

One of the best examples of the order versus chaos pattern is the story of Peter Pan and Wendy. Peter is the Boy Who Won't Grow Up, the embodiment of childish enthusiasm, spontaneity, mischief and fun, a stealer of bikes. He is the leader of a pack of other Lost Boys with whom he lives in Neverland. Peter represents a life without any real adult responsibilities. He may be a leader, but he is not a Father nor a provider. He has no desire to sign contracts, to make long commitments, to settle down, because something wonderful might be just around the corner. He has a deep fear of being trapped, netted, buried alive. His dilemma is his desire for love and a Mother for himself and his boys versus his need to always keep moving, to remain unattached. The downside of this free existence is that he must trade the joys of participation in a mature emotional and intellectual life for his freedom. He is stuck on the horns of a dilemma.

Wendy is the young girl whom Peter abducts from her staid but loving and warm Victorian home in London along with her two younger brothers. She is a civilized young woman on the very brink of womanhood. While she is desperately drawn to Peter's child world, she needs to live warmly wrapped in the hearts of her family, to be able to predict future happiness, to have an orderly place in which she can flower. Wendy wants a house around her to protect her and a reliable partner who will love and cherish her and her children. She values manners and security, but as a young girl, she is caught between the desire to stay a child and the need to grow up. She must trade freedom and childhood for adult responsibilities. Her reward for this will be true adult love and intellectual growth.

Peter's stated intention in Wendy's abduction is to provide a Mother for the Lost Boys. Wendy happily goes along with this, and she and her brothers proceed to settle into an adventurous and carefree life in Neverland. Trouble starts brewing rather quickly between Peter and Wendy because of their opposing needs. Peter wants to be taken care of, but *not* tamed, not domesticated; Wendy wants to have fun, but *not* at the expense of growing up and love. The essential order vs. chaos conflict shared by almost all stories is easily exposed.

Peter attracts Wendy because he pushes her to fly and to adventure. He provides fun and excitement. Wendy attracts Peter because she nurtures him and looks up to him at the same time. Peters and Wendys need each other because without Wendy, Peter may simply fly out of orbit and never return, and Wendy may seal herself permanently in a house by the side of the road. Peter needs an anchor and Wendy needs a propeller. You may look to any relationship to see how this works. The easiest thing to ask yourself is "who keeps the checkbook?" When you find that out, you have found Wendy.

In the play, *The Three Sisters*, Olga, the eldest sister, will not quickly give up her need to order the family's life simply because her brother brings home a less-than-acceptable bride and her baby sister, Irina, finds a suitor. Her middle sister, Masha's, emotional relegation of responsibility to other members of the family will not soon change. It is probable that were we to write a story set five years after the end of *The Three Sisters* called *Olga in Moscow*, we would still find the family up to their same old patterns of relationships. These patterns have to do with responsibility versus spontaneity, just like Peter and Wendy.

Looking at one's own family, it is fairly easy to discern that patterns take many years to change if they ever do so at all. If you were to write a play about your own family named *Junior's Gay Marriage*, it wouldn't take much imagination to see how each family member would play a part; who would team with whom; who would arrange the caterer versus who would refuse to come; who would break down in tears at the wedding and who would be in the back of the church. The conflicts in the relationships, i.e., "Mom always loved you best," "You always think you are right," "You are absolutely incompetent at things like this," and all the other sibling and parental problems would come bursting out of the wedding ceremony.

Summation

The essential idea remains: It is the long-term conflict within the relationships that are ignited by the fire of the plot. Conflict that was hidden is brought to the fore; the story exists to talk about how we are with each other and how that leads to what we do to each other.

Notes

1 Eckerling, Debra. *Interview with Robert McKee*, August 18, 2009. http://www.storylink.com/article/321.
2 Hillman, James. (1990). Oedipus Variations: Studies in Literature and Psychoanalysis. *Spring Journal*, 90.
3 Coupe, Lawrence. *Kenneth Burke on Myth: An Introduction*. London: Routledge Press, 2005.
4 Courtesy of the Picasso Estate.

Part II

The exercises and the work

Chapter 4

The exercises

As theatre is a means of telling stories, perhaps a more efficient use of theatrical training is to reconnect to the larger-than-life original accounts of heroes, shamanistic performances, and archetypes that are the basis of virtually every story being told. Stories in all likelihood predate complex verbal language. Large vocabularies and written language came later as well as codified and elaborated meaning. Writing clarified and validated meaning while at the same time creating the belief in an actual and literal "know-ability" not present in the original and changeable oral presentations of these powerful tales and myths. Writing had the effect of eroding the mystery and magic that the myths formerly held.

I have created a group of exercises for use in rehearsals and in classes that culminate in what my students refer to as Superscenes. These offer a way to enable actors to work as an ensemble in truthful, impulsive, and theatrical ways while honoring both text and subtext as myth. This series of exercises is based in biology, mythology, anthropology, and neuroscience, and incorporates the thinking of Joseph Campbell, C.G. Jung, James Hillman, George Herbert Mead, Herbert Blumer, Ernest Becker, Antonio Damasio, Michael Gazzaniga, and V.S. Ramachandran as well as more traditional acting and directing pedagogy. The overall thrust of this book is my desire to aid actors, directors, and acting teachers to rediscover the thrill of performances that are physically, spiritually, emotionally, and intellectually exciting enough for the stage. My starting point is in the nature of storytelling, myth, and archetype. For me these elements are the constants in any performance medium. The exercises in this chapter are structured in such a way as to prepare the students for Superscenes, which will be discussed in Chapter 6.

Meditation: Opening the way

Teaching yogic meditation practice is one of the most useful skills a teacher can give to an acting student. Meditation can quiet a restless mind and release harmful self-consciousness. The word "yoga" can be translated to mean the act of hitching up a horse or an ox. In this case, meditation training enables the actor to yoke his or her mind and body with breath. In my own work, I employ a yoga teacher to do the physical aspect of yoga, as I am not trained in it. Ideally, the physical movement practice would precede seated meditation on the day of class.

Be careful to distinguish this practice from prayer; there will be some students whose religious leaders may regard meditation and Buddhist methods as antireligious activity. For those of us who use meditation and yoga regularly, it is easy to see that this is not true, but you may have students who are wary. In this case, I suggest that they simply try it out and make up their own minds. In the history of my teaching, none have opted out after discovering what this actually is.

Instructions

1 Ask students to sit quietly against a wall or cross-legged on the floor, if that is comfortable. Yoga mats are not needed for this work. For beginners, my suggestion is to allow them to sit as comfortably as possible; some may need to be in chairs, but most will be able to sit with their backs against a wall. All should aim for as straight a back as possible, with shoulders back and heads stacked on top of their spines. The position of their legs is up to the individual; some will sit in a traditional yogic cross-legged pose, but some will need to assume other positions for comfort. There should be no strain.

2 I suggest that once a position can be easily held, the participant imagine a spotlight above them, surrounding their body closely, beyond which they cannot be seen. I sometimes make a reference to Stanislavski's first circle of concentration at this point. Further, advise them to imagine a rope of energy

proceeding from the beginning of the spine and moving up and out through the skull toward the sky.

3   Once peace falls on the room, encourage the participants to release any tension, working from their feet to their head or in the reverse. Recommend that they soften their jaw by thrusting it forward and then letting it drop. Suggest that their eyes should be closed and relaxed. Later in the first week, I will suggest opening them and seeing but not looking; soft eyes, as Ann Bogart would name it. We can open eyes and find points of concentration later.

4   Instruct the actors to become aware of their breath without adjusting it, to simply focus on its rhythm and how it feels.

5   As they begin to do this, survey the room to check each student for tension or discomfort. If you see shoulders held high, or legs striving to hold a pose, walk up and whisper to the student that he or she should find a way of sitting that frees them from tension.

6   The next step is to ask the students to take three or four deep breaths, each breath going deeper as they enter into the meditative state.

7   The first several sessions should be limited to ten minutes, and as the practice becomes easier for everyone, the sessions can be lengthened. The students become very proud of themselves when they can do twenty or thirty minutes. As class time becomes more and more crowded with scenes, we can't always do the necessary meditation. I encourage the students to use the skill at home. It is surprising how many of them do so.

8   For the first seven days or so I incorporate imagistic spoken guidance leading their thoughts into nature. Sometimes I evoke the image of a soft warm wind blowing through a tree to move thoughts softly into the air, or of a leaf carrying thoughts down in a gently flowing stream. Frequently, I suggest silently saying hello and goodbye to intrusive thoughts. At times, I use the image of baby monkeys in the trees waking up and jumping up and down, screaming for attention, and suggest that the meditators rock them to sleep in the branches or warm them with a wind or whatever. I often emphasize the need to kindly welcome thoughts coming in the front gate while allowing them to move through the back gate. The idea is that thoughts are allowed to move through the woods but not set up camp. The object is to help the participant accept that thoughts will come and go

and don't need to dominate the brain. Total acceptance is the goal. A mentor in this activity must use his or her own imagination to create images of depth and clarity for the actors. It is a form of meditation for him or her as well.

Other suggestions

- Let your mind float up and out of the windows on the sound made by the heat or air conditioning in the room.
- When you feel an itch or the need to move, talk to it as you would to the baby monkeys in the trees.
- If a thought fascinates you, hang it on the tree for a further visit.
- Always return to your breath, and it will free you.

After the allotted time, if we are moving onto another exercise, i.e., Viewpoints, or Sticks, I ask the students to slowly stand, rolling up their spines while keeping eyes closed. As this is accomplished, I instruct the actors to slowly open their eyes, and, using soft focus, to begin the next exercise quietly with no social interaction. If we are moving to a discussion or a scene, I often ask that they briefly report what their experience in the meditation had been. Each person must participate. This discussion helps create ensemble quickly, generally with a lot of laughter of recognition.

Discussion

- Did you feel as if you had any moments of deep meditation?
- Were you working too hard?
- Were you able to accept noises in the room and outside it without upsetting your peace?
- Did anything new happen during today's session?

Magnets: Exploring visceral response

The object of the magnet exercise is to encourage awareness of the response felt in the actor's solar plexus when being approached and the different feelings engendered when "personal space" is transgressed. This simple activity enables actors to connect to their biology as something that is not solely passive and internal. As we are all aware, when someone approaches us on a sidewalk, we have some sort of gut response to the impending presence as the person nears.

There are four places where this feeling occurs: First, at about 30 feet, when we recognize that we will have to deal with an approaching figure and determine if he or she is friend or foe; second, between 10 and 15 feet when the figure is near enough that we need to either move to the side to avoid collision or continue moving directly ahead; third, at about 5 feet, when the figure encroaches on our personal space; and fourth, when the figure moves into our personal space, usually at 1 or 2 feet. This exercise in proximity will remind or awaken the participants to the physiological response to others. This proof of our biological connection to others is a building block for relationship.

Ingredients

Barefoot actors
A large space for movement
Two large magnets to demonstrate magnetism, if needed

Instructions

It is often interesting to demonstrate the attraction and repulsion using magnets and to emphasize the strength of both energies.

1   Have the actors line up opposite each other in two lines facing each other as far apart as possible. One line should be on the north or west side of the room and the other on the south or east side of the room. Doing this outdoors is optimal. The participants should take note of the distance between them and the partner directly across the space.

2   Instruct one line to move slowly toward the other and to stop when requested to do so by the person to whom they are moving.

3   The static line is instructed to call "stop" to the person moving toward them when their body signals to them that they are going to have to deal with the approaching person's presence in one way or another, just as they would have to do on the street. The stopping distance may vary from one person to another depending on cultural norms, gender, and personal preference, but it is usually around 10 or 15 feet if they are about 30 feet apart to

begin. (There will be some actors who don't signal stop until the partner approaching is very near. In my experience, such actors are trying to appear open and accepting and do not want to acknowledge the feeling of trepidation natural to any animal. When this occurs, I ask the couple to try again or change partners and for the static person to be more alert to his or her body). This must be done carefully to avoid the idea that the actors are somehow doing it wrong or are insufficient.

4   I then ask the moving line to advance once again slowly toward the person in front of them.

5   Again the static line is asked to call "stop" to their moving partner as the approach begins to feel somehow meaningful. This is usually between 5 and 7 feet in distance.

6   Now, suggest that the moving line transgress their partner's personal space. In general, most people will giggle or step back as a result of this encroachment. Depending on the class, I will often refer to this as the giggle space or the Fight or F**k space, because this proximity is generally limited to one of those activities. Allow the giggling; it is an important release and helps to balance the individuals. This can also be seen as fight or flight, but the freezing of a person in danger and the tension involved is in reality more natural than immediate fight or flight. I have found that foul language is a great aid to the memory of my students, but I use it sparingly.

7   The exercise repeats, allowing the formerly moving line to be static and the formerly static line to experience transgressing their opposite's space.

8   After this has been accomplished, I suggest that the partners experiment with keeping the F-or-F space between them as they move around the room in different configurations. First face-to-face, then side-to-side, then back-to-back. They will discover that back-to-back and face-to-face are easier than side-to-side because we don't have as much sensory awareness there. See how far they can maintain the sense of connection.

Sample side comments during the exercise

• How far can you distance yourselves from one another and still feel the connection?

• Can you maintain it with your backs? Your sides?

• Can you stretch it or compress it?

• Imagine it as a silver balloon connecting you with invisible rays to your partner.

Push, pull, hold, release: Essential actions

This exercise was created through my understanding of renowned acting theoretician, director, and teacher Paul Kassel's ideas of "push, pull, hold, and release" (PPHR) as the basic elements of action, whether expressed or repressed. This idea originated with Jacques LeCoq, but Kassel's take on it is the one I prefer. This concept emphasizes cooperation between actors as well as sensory work. Additionally, it illustrates that all actions, however described, emerge from the simple act of pushing and pulling either figuratively, literally, or physically and that the communication of the hold and release is vital to new action. Once again, my aim is to unearth the primal beneath language. Kassel's books include *Acting: An Introduction to the Art and Craft of Playing*, 2007.[1]

Ingredients

A large floor
Barefoot actors

Instructions

1   Assign partners two by two and ask them to face one another with soft focus.
2   Demonstrate, using a student, what it looks like to push someone *to something*, or to push away *from something*. Repeat with *pulling away* and *pulling toward*. Mention that violent shoving or sudden grabs and pulls should be avoided.
3   Have the students experiment with these movements sequentially.

    • Push to: Begin from the back of the person being pushed
    • Push from: Again from the back
    • Pull to: From the front
    • Pull from: Again from the front

4   Once this is done, and as you observe the naturally occurring stops and starts that will occur, introduce the idea of "hold," wherein the participants stop, make eye contact, breathe, and take in their partner. Emphasize that this is a "hold," neither a stop nor a rest.

5 At the same time offer the idea of "hold and release" as a natural way of handling any situation and moving forward to something new. The same energy should be present; neither the hold nor the release should be an actual stoppage of breath or energy. This is the same idea experienced in yoga physical practice. The energy in the "hold" is converted into the "release," which is once again *not* a point of relaxation. This exercise seems very easy at first, but the teacher and the students should closely observe the desire to physically drop out of the game during the hold and release.

6 Let the actors play with using different parts of their bodies or different postures, perhaps pushing with one finger, or with the head or foot, or pulling with a knee or by sitting on the floor and surrounding a partner's ankles with their legs.

7 Once this is accomplished, ask the students to move around the room trying to project and use the actions of push/pull/hold/release with no physical touch. How far apart can they be and still affect each other? Can they employ other parts of their bodies metaphorically? For instance, an actor could imagine butting his head into someone's belly.

Discussion

- When the actors were pushing, did they envision a destination without consciously deciding on one, or was it a conscious decision?
- How did the destination affect the movement?
- Introduce the idea that *action frequently precedes reasoning* and that humans find it difficult to do anything for too long without a story attaching to it.
- Emphasize that the hold and the release may be the most useful moments in the scene because they not only keep the actors in concert, but the suspense and the communication are rich at that time.
- What does "PPHR" have to do with "beats"?

Sticks: Conflict and cooperation

This very enjoyable activity enables an actor to connect to his or her partner as someone who must be confronted and engaged with mutually. It elicits focus on both partner and outside elements. It resonates in scenes because once actors have played this game, they feel permanently linked to each other sensorially. It also trains the body to work spontaneously, vigorously, and joyfully. It can be done in rehearsal for scene work as well.

The simple design of the stick work is sequential, moving from no actual personal contact to deep interpersonal communication. It is also a means for the participants to experience the floor and become aware of the many sensory contacts available through the feet. In doing so, the actor becomes grounded. Many of the elements can be found in the brilliant work of James LeCoq, master teacher, and in Viewpoints (see the next exercise), although Schranz originated these exercises without an awareness of them. My own feeling is that the two live well together.

There is no way that I can fully describe the entirety of this brilliant device developed by Schranz, and hopefully he will fully publish his work, including not only this exercise but several others, among them Strings, as well as his method of creating performance without bosses.

Ingredients

Barefoot actors

A space large enough for actors to move freely, such as a dance studio, a gym, etc.

Enough sticks for each couple to share one. (These sticks must be stiff with no bend, something like dowels or plastic plumbing pipe. It is best if they measure 4 feet long by 1¼ inch in diameter. Use some padding on each end. We use a cut up sponge covered with duct tape and a piece of Velcro or other rough material on top of the ends).

Instructions

1 Split the participants into pairs.
2 Present each team with a stick.
3 Each member of the pair puts the stick at a point on their abdomen slightly above their groin. This point is about three-quarters

of the way below the belly button and one quarter above the groin. There is a reason for the padding! Often this is difficult for beginners, and as long as the stick is at least two inches below the belly button, I don't complain.

4   Once the sticks are held lightly between the two, the actors are instructed to look only at the place where the stick meets their partner's body.

5   The actors are then asked to move around the room without pushing overly much but reading the subtler clues given to them through the stick and their feet. They are prompted to keep their heels down and to have active toes, awareness of foot placement, to fully experience the feelings in their feet and to do so without excess tension.

Sidecoaching

Make sure that the actors know that there is absolutely no penalty for dropping the stick, and that, should it fall, they should simply pick it up and go on.

- Comment to individual members of the class with such things as "release your hands" or "let your face be as loose as it was when you first woke up today" or "use your feet without tensing your arms." This should be done publicly in order to assure others that adjustments are not shameful and must be made.

- Emphasize that this activity should begin in a meditative way and then move into an outward consciousness as the game expands.

- If the student is flat-footed, encourage rolling through the right foot and pushing off from its big toe as the left foot remains still. (Flat-footed walkers don't roll; they plod forward even though they may not actually have fallen arches.) When the right heel lifts, make sure that only the *toes* of the right foot are on the floor. The right foot should move forward and land on the heel as the left and right feet orchestrate the procedure. (I also suggest that these folks play with picking up small things using their feet. It is fun!)

6   The first moves that the partners attempt should be backwards and forwards at a slow to medium pace and then, as soon as possible, to an "established fast and an established slow

rhythm," varying between the two suddenly with no medium. This is similar to the upcoming exercise using Viewpoints in the differentiation between tempos with sudden changes, if possible. My sidecoaching is generally, "Don't bore yourselves."

7 As soon as the pairs seem to be somewhat adept, add sideways movements, using the established tempos, and encourage the pair to cover the entire floor without bumping into others.

8 Once this is accomplished, the two are instructed to focus on each other's sternums as they move and, after a while, on foreheads.

9 Then, as in Magnets and yoga, the actors are invited to stop or start with the codicil that their stops and starts must be fully energized without any rest. As Schranz says, "The energy for the stop must be in the start and the energy for the start must be in the stop."

10 As this becomes easier, the pairs are invited to look into their partner's eyes, first casually and then with as much intensity as possible without tension. Schranz calls this "Laser Vision."

11 From here on, actors are encouraged to play freely with tempo and space while keeping the stick between them and to add in whatever jumps or squats they wish to do.

12 By this time, there will be lots of giggling, laughing, or grunting, because the game is so much fun.

13 As the actors become accustomed to the game, it is time to add "reference points." A reference point is any place in the room on a wall or door or any architectural feature that can be seen by one of the participants. Partner A may say, "My reference point is the fire alarm," and the other may say, "Mine is that dirty speck near the door." It is best if these points are not on the same wall. Once a reference point is chosen, the actor must split his or her laser-like visual focus between the point and the partner. The point must be as much a *magnet* as is the partner. The reference point becomes a second partner, beckoning, trapping, threatening, and so on to be either avoided or approached.

14 After a while, the actors are asked to relinquish their sticks and do the same exercise with a virtual stick, paying particular attention to the reference point even when they are forced to turn their backs on each other to reach it. My sidecoaching is usually, "Don't change the size of the stick."

15 Now, invite the participants to add another reference point, and then another, and another, each time dividing the actor's

focus. These additional reference points can either push or pull on the actor and now must be imagined as if occurring at specific place on the actor's body, e.g., one point pulling at the heel and another pushing on the back of the head.

16 While these elements are being added, the mentor must continue to encourage physical lack of tension, strong focus, and varied tempos and dynamics.

I end with the statement given to us by Schranz, "Be faithful to what the stick has taught you."

Discussion

- What did you discover?
- What was new for you?
- What did you learn about yourself?
- What did you learn about your partner?
- Does this exercise have anything to do with magnets?
- How is push/pull/hold/release used in sticks?
- What do the reference points do to you?
- What do they mean?

Viewpoints

Viewpoints technique was first developed by the postmodern choreographer Mary Overlie as a way of deconstructing and defining the essential constituents of movement in time and space. She created a vocabulary called Viewpoints because it examined elemental movement from six different perspectives. Ann Bogart and Tina Landau expanded the number of viewpoints to twelve to be more helpful for actors and directors. The practice of Viewpoints is a means of training actors in spontaneity, physical commitment, ensemble building, sensory awareness, self-discovery, and embodied creativity. This terminology is an important piece of acting training in the twenty-first century.

Ingredients

At least six barefoot actors
A clear space – large enough for each actor to be able to run freely is optimal

Bogart's viewpoints

Tempo
Duration
Repetition
Kinesthetic Response
Shape
Gesture
Architecture
Spatial Relationship
Topography
Pitch
Volume
Timbre

It is not my practice to utilize the vocal viewpoints, pitch, volume, timbre very often, although I do refer to them in rehearsal and scene work. Teachers and directors of Viewpoints must find their own way through them and use them as desired, and in the order they appear appropriate during the exercises themselves. The only essential for me is to begin with tempo on the grid.

Viewpoints can be done at any point in the exercise line up, but I find it most helpful to do them in a separate session from other exercises and begin with meditation.

Instructions: First viewpoints class

1   Establish the boundaries of the grid determined by the size of the room and the number of the students. There needs to be about 18 to 24 inches of space from each wall for the participants to be "off the grid." I frequently reference the tiles on the ceiling or on the floor as a means of indicating the grid. Creating these boundaries is important because they frame the space through limitation, an essential concept of artistic creation. Off the grid is a relaxation place; on the grid is where the work is done.

2   Request that the actors who have been meditating rise from their meditation and attempt to keep the peace of it in their bodies and in their eyes.

3   Suggest to walk aimlessly within the grid, making no eye contact but imagining looking through the walls or out the windows.

Soft eyes helps to encourage less reliance on sight and puts more dependence on other senses.

4   As the group members walk, instruct them to walk only north, south, east, or west, on the grid. The class should be prompted to avoid curves and only work in right angles. As this goes on, the students will become quiet and attentive simply to their movement.
5   Alert the participants that one of their objectives is "never be bored."
6   Once most actors seem to have found a contemplative approach to moving, take a short break for water and rest.

Sidecoaching

*   Pay attention to your breath as you walk, and keep a meditative flow if possible.
*   Release any tension.
*   Maintain soft eyes.
*   Stay on the grid.
*   Don't bore yourself.

The first three viewpoints – tempo, duration, repetition

1   Invite the actors back to moving on the grid and allow them to settle into the space once more.
2   Suggest that they move in the following ways:

    *   Imperceptibly slowly
    *   Extremely fast
    *   Medium
    *   Medium fast
    *   Medium slow

The object for the performer in doing this is to recognize and establish the differences in the energy/concentration required by each speed.

Sidecoaching

*   Call out different tempos in quick succession or at random times.
*   Simply clap hands to signal a change in pace without dictating what it should be. This begins to pull the actor out of conscious choice and into impulse.
*   Encourage maintaining soft focus, examining energy flow, and emphasizing the idea that the participant should never be

bored. This is a novel idea for most, and needs to be reiterated because it takes the focus off of pleasing the instructor and encourages the students to play for themselves.

The prior section of the exercise can take about twenty minutes. At this time, there may be a need to get off the grid at least psychologically and break for water and rest.

Discussion

- What did you observe in your own body as you changed tempos?
- Did you find yourself stuck or bored?
- Were you able to clearly distinguish between tempos?
- How and where was your energy in each tempo?

3   After the actors are recovered, invite them back onto the grid and into the state of being that it requires. Allow them to play with tempos and introduce the idea that they may choose to "stop" or "start," which is a new element in the exercise.

4   Emphasize that the flow of energy should be maintained and that "stopping" should not be resting or dropping out, just as in magnets and sticks. Let the group play with this idea. This is a "hold and release" concept from the PPHR exercise discussed earlier.

5   The actors' menus now include varied tempos as well as stops and starts. As they continue, add the idea that they can now leap or squat or do a combination of those moves as long as the stops and starts remain constant in the energy levels. These new options can be a big step and it is important that they be done *efficiently and silently*.

When leaping, the actors should keep their legs behind them almost as if they were kicking themselves in the butt. Landings must be silent and the energy controlled.

6   As these movement possibilities are presented, it is time to offer the concepts of *duration* (how long one does something) and *repetition* (repeating something) as another way of increasing physical awareness and meaning. Let the class play with these ideas. Be aware that repetition can be seen as boring unless it is mindfully done.

This is generally where I end the first class in Viewpoints; however, my classes may be longer than yours. The actors should be tired but not exhausted.

Discussion

- What did you observe in your own body as you changed tempos?
- Did you find yourself stuck or bored?
- Were you able to clearly distinguish between tempos?
- How and where was your energy in each tempo?
- Were you able to surprise yourself?

Instructions: Second viewpoints class – contact and company

After meditation, once again invite everyone to begin working on the grid using all the tools they have been given. Encourage exploration of habitual movement and changes possible within it. This should take about twenty minutes.

Sidecoaching

- Encourage doing "the next right thing," logical or not.
- Urge the participants to use other parts of their bodies to move, perhaps to scoot on the floor or crawl or roll or tiptoe or lead with their knees or noses. Invite fearless silliness seriously.
- Remind them that medium is the least fun thing to do.
- If they haven't already discovered going backwards, make that suggestion.
- Discourage boredom.

Take a five-minute break with water and not a lot of communication, and then back to the grid.

Introduce kinesthetic response

The last exercise of the day, and probably the most difficult and enlightening, is *kinesthetic* response. The major instruction is that whenever an actor passes another person or is passed by another person, the actor must instantly physically change whatever they are doing. Changing speeds is important here for the instructor. At first this will be overwhelming; we are asking the performers to embrace chaos. However, with enough encouragement, the actors will be forced to give up holding onto any preconceptions and enter the world of freedom and spontaneity.

1   Invite the participants back onto the grid and to establish a medium-fast walk, soft eyes. Allow them to do this for only a few minutes and then ask the class to begin changing as they pass or are passed by others. Let this go on for about five minutes depending on the needs of the individuals in the group. Make sure you are calling changes yourself when you see actors not changing. Don't fear frustrating people or calling out an individual name.

2   As the actors move on the grid, they will already have been discovering that it is difficult to go it alone and will unconsciously be drawn to working with others.

3   Now suggest that the actors move together in pairs and adopt each other's movements rather than beginning new ones. The idea here is to follow the follower.

This pairing should not be assigned; it should be random and change rapidly. The partnerships should morph their movement without consultation, as should instantly begin doing the same thing. So two people may be walking in the same tempo and swinging arms up over their heads at the same time. This can change as the dynamic changes. They may slow down, speed up, lower their arms, but all must aim to happen at the same time. Again, no leader, no follower.

4   As they travel, support the idea that the tandem movements may change spontaneously, and that individuals may split off to another duo. If someone comes into an existing duo, one of the pair must leave and team up elsewhere. Avoid trios at this point. The activity of the duos must be maintained and morph regardless of a change in partners. All must aim to happen at the same time. Again, no leader, no follower. The joining partner must join and adjust in the same way that the departing partner must join and adjust to another partner.

5   As this activity goes forward, remind the group that medium anything incites boredom. Play with this using not only tempo but also duration and repetition. The instructor must be aware that calling changes a bit faster than the class may seem to be able to handle will finally allow many of the participants to "get out of their heads."

6   Continue these encounters, suggesting that the students move in threesomes, then foursomes, and so on.

7   Introduce the idea that whenever on group passes another, the entire group must instantly physically change whatever they are doing as a group.

8   Suggest that all leap at the same time, or squat at the same time, or run, or stop, or sit. At first this will be difficult, but miraculously it works out, to the joy of everyone. This company-building exercise is one of the best I have ever encountered. I often suggest that the group members think of themselves as a herd of deer as they move freely on the grid, and that suddenly one of the deer spots a mountain lion and signals everyone to freeze and notice. The participants should be encouraged to start and stop at the same time. This scenario offers many variations, and I don't have space to list them; find them for yourselves and have a good time.

9   Suggest that they are all on the edges of a very, very large round platter. Surrounding the platter is a moat filled with hungry crocodiles. The only problem is that the platter rests on a large rubber ball in the center and if the balance is lost, all will slide into the moat. The object of this game is to continue moving while maintaining the balance needed for the safety of all. Actors should take into account their own size, speed, distance, and the other variables that might result in disaster.

Sidecoaching

- Change! Now!
- Give up and go with it!
- Don't forget tempo, duration, repetition!
- Avoid medium!
- Don't let the crocodiles get you!
- Feel free to join others with tactics!

Take a short break for water and recovery!

Discussion

- How was that for you?
- What did you discover?
- What did you enjoy?
- Did you surprise yourself?
- How might this relate to a play or scene?
- What do you know about control?
- Were you bored?

Instructions: Company, architecture, and music

Begin on the grid, and when the actors are ready, suggest that they use the architecture of the room as an impetus for movement and exploration. Mention the concept of reference points from the Sticks exercise. Suggest that they move using the textures, the vagaries of the woodwork, the walls, the chairs, the bags, and anything else in the room. They can do this individually or in groups as the exercise morphs. I often suggest that they "dance off" the environment. Discourage too much isolation. You may see actors who are fearful of relationships move to objects or corners and get stuck there.

You might want to recommend that the actors work on the grid with their eyes closed. This allows the actors to feel the light filtering through their eyelids and feel the heat given off by the other bodies in the room. It is usually best to work with a stage manager or assistant director to function as a shepherd with you for those who wander like lost sheep. There will be collisions, but allow them to occur and counsel the participants to accept them in the same way they accepted the dropping of sticks.

Sidecoaching

- Don't be afraid; we will not let you hurt yourself.
- Move toward the light even if you can't see it.
- Where is the heat in the room?
- Free yourself of unnecessary tension.
- Trust and walk fearlessly.
- Do you want to join someone?

On this day, I frequently play a variety of unfamiliar instrumental music from classical to jazz, pop, and tribal. Vocals encourage too much literal work. I encourage the actors on the grid to move as the music plays in any way they desire while maintaining viewpoints, either singly or in groups. Do not allow this to become a dance piece. It has far more to do with the shape of the music, its tone and texture, playing both with and against the rhythm with and without partners or groups.

I may reintroduce the concept of reference points investigated in 'Sticks' at this time. If I am working on a particular text, I may choose music from the period or style suggested by it. This is also a good time to change from linear movements to curves and circles, which will excite many of the participants. Again, caution must be taken with curves to ensure that the dancers in the group don't suddenly begin to do structured dance. It can be too easy for them, and their bodies will feedback in expected ways.

Sidecoaching

- What is the shape of this music?
- What color?
- How do the reference points change?
- What does the tempo mean to you?
- Are you always moving using only your feet?
- Can you use your elbows? Shins? Little fingers?
- Do you need to be with the rhythm or can you move in a counterpoint?
- If you like someone else's moves, feel free to join, but don't bore yourself.

Note

1 Paul Kassel. *Acting: An Introduction to the Art and Craft of Playing.* New York: Pearson, 2007.

Chapter 5

Beginning Superscenes

Text and archetypes

Before beginning physical Superscenes, the cast should do a close reading of the play. (It is assumed that if they are going to present the show, they will already have read the text prior to the first full-cast rehearsal.) Perhaps this should be called a "read-in" rehearsal rather than a "read through." It should take about three evenings or three four-hour stretches of work. You may consider that the first two sessions are for the deep read and the third session as a time to put it together. Time should not be rushed and must allow for lots of discussion of themes, myths, symbols, and the playwright's worldview and previous work, as well as the given circumstances of the play. Discussion should *discourage* examination of characters or their psychology. However, table work beyond three days can be detrimental to spontaneous work on the part of the actors, create too much of a hierarchical relationship with the director, and, finally, bore those actors who want to get up and get rid of "all that talk." You will have time to cover things in rehearsal.

It is a good idea for everyone – directors, designers, actors, stage managers, assistant directors, assistants to the assistants – to bring lots of images, as well as myth and archetype books from different cultures for the students to peruse or borrow (of course, be careful, they might not return them). I generally have the books and images posted in the room from the beginning until the end of the rehearsal process.

Discussion for first reading day

Following each *scene* ask the following questions:

- If this scene weren't in the play, what would be different?
- Who wasn't in the scene?

- Was there someone influencing the scene who was not in it?
- Who won?
- What actually occurred?

At the end of each *act* ask the following questions:

- Who won?
- What has to happen next?
- Who is this play about primarily?

Assignment

Even though they have not finished reading the play on the first day, ask each actor to begin doing some myth and archetype research on the story and specifically the role they are playing in it. I have at times requested that this be done before the first read to encourage thinking on a mythic scale. Suggest how they might Google the information and offer books for them to use. My method is simply to search such things as "god who abandons his family" or "mythology in Ibsen" or "goddess with wings."

Designers and dramaturgs usually use the first day of rehearsal for presentations. My experience is that this is wasted time because the cast is too anxious to actually attend to the presentations. I believe that the fourth or fifth day is better used for that activity because the actors will have some way to connect to whatever the designers and dramaturgs are saying and will not feel the power structure on top of them.

Discussion for second day

Ask the same scene questions as on the first day for the remainder of the play.

At the end of the *full play* reading, ask the following questions:

- Who won?
- What is not resolved?
- Why does this play exist?
- Why should we do it? For whom?
- What is the essential conflict of this play, i.e., Responsibility to family versus Self-actualization?
- Who in this play represents order? Who, chaos?
- If this play were a fairy tale, what would it be?
- What film or TV show might this be?

- What myth or myths seem to be the basis of the play?
- Who is the protagonist? Who, the antagonist?
- What does the protagonist do to the antagonist to win?
- What does the antagonist do to the protagonist to win?
- Does either of them win? Or, does either of them lose? Or is it a draw?

This discussion of the play enables the actors to fully participate and to understand what they must do for the play to fulfill its trajectory. It makes them partners in the endeavor and eliminates many rehearsal problems.

Third or fourth day: Exercise: Using the monomyth

At the beginning of the class or rehearsal, the circular Hero's Journey should be on a blackboard or some large surface, and the actors should be given a printed copy of it along with their scripts so that they can talk about the journey of the play. *Emphasize that*

Figure 5.1 Circular Hero's Journey

Adele Cerda, A Cerda Design, www.acerdadesign.com.

every person is the hero or protagonist of his or her own life and that we all can look at our own lives in the same way. All the characters in the play are on a journey that, when viewed from their particular perspective, is no less important to them. All of the actors need to discover where they (their character) are on their journey, realizing that it is quite probable that the only complete journey revealed in the play may be that of the protagonist and/or antagonist. Some may say that their 'character' remains the same. Given what we know of the chemistry of change, this is not feasible. The journey may be slight, it may be hidden, but it will be there somewhere. I like to say that the journey highlighted in this particular story reveals the chosen protagonist's journey, and that each character will in turn be chosen to be the protagonist of the metaphoric next series concerning the world of the play. I always insist that the students to refer to their "character" as "I." If used well enough, it can keep them intellectually honest.

It is simplest to first do this exercise from the actual dramatic protagonist's point of view. If there is any question as to who the protagonist is, it can be easily discovered, because the protagonist and that antagonist should be still on the stage in the final scene of the play. If they are not, you might be stuck with some really long denouement! I refer you to the excellent book *Backwards and Forwards* by David Ball for a longer look at this idea.

A circular representation of the Hero's Journey

You must be aware that the journey may be stopped along the way, may not include each step, or may circle back and repeat at times. There is also a Female Hero's Journey, but I have rarely found it as useful as the original Journey as expressed by Joseph Campbell. My other piece of advice is for the reader to realize that the journey may be completely external, as in an action movie, or it may be completely internal, as in many Bergman films.

There are three examples of Hero's Journeys in this book; those of Hamlet and Muhammad Ali in Chapter 6 and the character of Hester from Suzan Lori-Parks's play *In The Blood*, Chapter 10.

Here is a brief linear description of the Hero's Journey.

A linear representation of the Hero's Journey

The Innocent World of Childhood: The hero is unaware that his or her life will be changed.

Call to Adventure: The hero is beckoned to change.

Refusal of the Call: The hero stalls and decides against attempting to leave his or her comfort zone.

The Magical Aid: The hero is helped by another person or circumstance and decides to take the journey.

Crossing the Threshold: The hero enters into uncomfortable and unfamiliar territory.

Belly of the Whale: The hero is stuck for a time before escaping this figurative or metaphoric place of inaction. He or she may also be rescued by an external person or force.

Road of Trials: The hero sets foot on the journey and moves from trial to trial.

Tests and Ordeals: The hero is severely tested; a dragon battle may ensue.

Symbolic Death and Dismemberment: The hero gives up his former life entirely and, in so doing, becomes a new person.

Meeting the Goddess: The hero meets with a feminine presence as a means of making peace with his or her own feminine side.

Atonement with or Recognition by the Father: The hero meets with a masculine presence as a means of making peace with his or her own masculine side.

The Ultimate Boon: The hero receives a gift, sometimes an actual object or sometimes new knowledge.

Apotheosis: The hero becomes Godlike. In having been born again and in having fully accepted all sides of his or her persona, the hero achieves wisdom and spiritual healing.

Refusal of the Return: The hero may hesitate to re-enter his or her former world.

The Magic Flight: A helper or a circumstance forces the hero to return home magically.

Crossing the Return Threshold: The hero returns home and commits to resuming life, albeit in an altered way.

Master of the Two Worlds: Having taken the journey, the hero has become able to deal with both the new world and the old one.

The actions of the scenes will usually be hooked to the Hero's Journey. For instance, the first scene in a play will invariably begin with the

World of Innocence and end with a Call to Adventure. This is generally true regardless of the drama's form. You will find that the journey becomes fairly easy to ascertain in this way. Even *Waiting for Godot* follows it, if you look carefully. This process will also help you as a teacher or a director to make sure that the scene has a dramatic arc, because the actors involved will understand the reason for its existence.

Additionally, the circular concept helps each actor determine whether his or her character finishes the journey or stops at a particular place and where that place is *spiritually*. So if an actor says, "Well, all she wants is the money in this scene," suggest that plays are rarely about money, which is literally a coin of exchange. The scene depends on *who* gives her the money and *who* the people are in it, so if the woman's scene is with her mother, you might ask, "Is it possible that you think you want money but you really need comfort or your mother's love or to finally have your mother give you something of value or . . . fill in the blank?" The teacher, casting director, playwright, and author of the book *Audition: Everything You Need To Know To Get The Part*, Michael Shurtleff, often said, "The character may not know what they need, but the actor must know."

The need of the characters must be sufficient to sustain them through all of the steps of the journey, and only other humans can help in the pursuit. Actors trying to find their "character" without actually deciding what they must do in the play or what they desperately need might say something like, "He is a jerk and all he wants is to kill his employer." In addition to warning the actors against such judgments, you might say, "Ok, he is a jerk, fine, but what does he NEED in order to grow as a full human being in this play?" Perhaps you might ask, "Does killing your boss turn out to be a relief or a curse?" And for the woman concerned with getting the money, "How will you grow if money is the object?" Many of the characters in the play will be defeated, but they should not go down because their NEED is too small. They should fail because they cannot sustain the fight, or because they drop out of it, or because they are overcome with fear, or because they are defeated by a power greater than they can fight.

Finally, the pursuit of character independent of the needs of the play will hopefully be stymied until such time as the actor, the god, and the given circumstances collide and merge. It is important that the actors begin to perceive that, in Sanford Meisner's words, "The play is not about what the play's about."[1] Once the performers begin to understand the importance of the internal and the external journey, literalness will subside, and the idea of subtext will naturally begin to emerge.

The discussion of the monomyth should be very lively, and there will be a lot of wrong turns. Allow the wrong turns and let the cast find them logically as you question them Socratically. Maybe you are wrong yourself! Allow the discussion to aid *you*; sometimes actors know more than directors or teachers. Do not be afraid to be seen learning. There should be a lot of erasures and restarts in this process. Once the protagonist journey is agreed upon, it's time for crafts! The actors must delineate the journey of their own characters either on a large sheet of paper or a portion of the blackboard big enough for the other actors to visit and see. I keep a roll of butcher paper in my office for this purpose. As they work, you may have to walk around the room and give aid and comfort! It will be noisy, confused, and frustrating. I have written a small paragraph on frustration that I usually give to a cast at the top of rehearsals. It is based on flow theory, developed by the idea of Mihaly Csikszentmihalyi.[2]

> The flow of learning proceeds from Frustration to Mastery to Boredom and back to Frustration in a continual upward moving spiral encompassing greater and greater circumference. Frustration therefore is to be desired and Mastery should be considered a transitory state. The circumference encircles more and more of the world of ideas and spiritual understandings in our dance of consciousness.

Having discussed the steps on the journey concerning the protagonist of the play in question, the actors are asked to consider the dilemma of their own role and to research a god or hero from any culture whose being personifies the tools and desires of their character. This is not about the actor's perception of the character's *identity*; it is about *the actions that they do* in the play. This is usually an exciting time for the actors as they discover the key to the story and the role in myth. They are often amazed and energized to see the bones emerge. A focus of this is to involve the actors in such a way that they become partners in the project rather than participants dependent upon the teacher or director for the answers to many questions.

Each actor must chart his or her scenes in relationship to what happens in the mythic chart. Each scene is examined and hooked to one of the elements of the journey. This should be done quickly and without much textual debate. We are looking for the larger events of the scene, not the beats, nor the lines themselves. The question must always be, "What happens?"

Once having made a stab at this exercise, the actors are encouraged to walk around and look at everyone else's charts to debate and discover where the roles intersect and what the interchange must be. Not only does this enable the actors to see the structure of the play, it also solidifies the idea that the cast owns the play and that they are responsible for each other in making sure that the steps along the way are accomplished.

We then finish the examination of the play by working to further define the protagonist and the antagonist of the play and how they play out the conflict textually using the simple protagonist/antagonist form provided on the next pages. Most of these answers are already understood, but it is nice to have an agreed-upon statement to refer to when things get difficult. *This idea should lead to a similar statement on the part of the individual actors, with the concept that every human is the protagonist of his or her own play.*

Protagonist/Antagonist Breakdown

Root Action
This root action should be present in every scene in some way.[3]

1 **Who?** *The protagonist-* (the person in the play who goes on the longest and most difficult journey)
2 **Needing what?**
3 **Does what** to the antagonist?
   BUT
4 **Who?** *The antagonist-* (the person who presents the protagonist with the hardest obstacles)
5 **Needing what?**
6 **Does what** to the protagonist?
7 **Resulting in what?**

Example:

Betty, needing to have someone who loves her unconditionally, gives all her heart, her soul, and her worldly possessions to Bob.

But:

Bob, needing to be worshipped and therefore held free of all responsibilities, bargains with Betty to accept friendship with sex rather than an all-encompassing love.

Resulting in:

> *Betty learning that she needs to respect herself enough to find a lover who will cherish and commit to her, and Bob's rejection of Betty in order to remain free. There are many myths behind this particular scenario, consider the Greek stories involving Echo and Narcissus, or Clytie and Helios.*

Exercise

My teacher and friend John Kirk formulated the Protagonist/Antagonist Breakdown included here. I have tried many other analytical tools, but I still come back to this one because of its insistence that the play revolves around conflicts in the relationships and their contribution to the theme or argument of the play, not the other way around.

Once cast members have determined their journeys, it is time to get even more specific and find the structure of the scenes.

For this exercise, please ask the student to indicate the scene and write the line or action (if it is indicated in the text itself, i.e., "He shoots his friend") wherein the following elements occur for the antagonist and the protagonist. The protagonist and antagonist will generally share this structure if the occurrence is strong enough.[4] If not, there may be an underlying structural problem, or the examination has not gone deep enough.

Inciting incident: Exact scene? Exact line? Rationale?

The inciting incident is the point in the early part of the play when we identify the protagonist and the antagonist because of something they have done. While many will postulate that the inciting incident predates the play's first act, it is best for all concerned to find exactly where and when it happens in the text itself. This is a point where audience members may nod and say, "Okay, I see what this is about."

The crisis: Exact scene? Exact line? Rationale?

The crisis is the point of conflict in the play where it is obvious that things are going to hit the fan sooner or later. I believe the audience members here often can be heard to say, "Uh oh" or "I don't want to see this!"

The catastrophe: Exact scene? Exact line? Rationale?

The catastrophe is the point at which things hit the fan. I often think that this is the place where certain audience members will vocalize "Oh No!" or some scatological language.

The climax: Exact scene? Exact line? Rationale?

The climax is the point at which the conflict in the plot is over, even though the conflict in the relationship remains essentially unsolved. The audience in this case will usually think something like, "Well, that is what had to happen!"

The denouement. Not usually exact unless it is tying up a subplot.

In a good piece of writing, after the climax, there should be no more than a few lines of denouement. If you decide that it is longer, check that you are putting your climax at the most intense or exciting action of the piece rather than at the resolution of the action.

This analysis can be done for a scene or an act or a play. It is the essential shape of dramatic writing. The root conflict and the root action *will not change essentially in the relationships.* If they do, the root has not been found. The plot structure is the place where story change takes place; it is situational and therefore changeable. However, the relational element, wherein the actor's deeper conflict is found, is rarely changeable. Just remember: the plot is *situational;* the conflict for the actor is *relational.*

Example:

(Little Red Riding Hood)
   (*needing to take her place in the world as an independent adult woman*) ventures into the forest (*a place of transformation*) and rebels against her mother's warnings to leave the path by befriending the Big Bad Wolf
   But
(The Big Bad Wolf)
   (*needing to guard his kingdom from human civilization*) lures Red Riding Hood through the forest and eats both Red and her Grandmother, resulting in the rebirth (*or transformation*) of Little Red, Grandma, and the death of the King Wolf.

The story of Red Riding Hood is at least a thousand years old, which may qualify it for myth rather than just fairy tale. It exists not only in Europe but also in countries as far spread as Australia,

Korea, Africa, and China under different guises. It rarely has a happy ending for Little Red, who personifies innocence and pluck. She is the flower about to bloom, but tough and resilient. As a woman, Little Red must be reborn as a creature of nature; her fertility must instate itself.

If this were a myth, it might be compared to: Hades's abduction of Persephone. What if Red Riding Hood were actually ravished by the Wolf, as Hades rapes Persephone, and what if she stayed and became like the wolf as Persephone does; what would the story mean then? What if Red didn't survive? What if Red ate her own grandmother, as in several versions of the story? Cannibalism and werewolves haunt the story. Blood is all over it: The red blood of death and menstruation.

The archetype of the maiden is basic to myth, as is the Shape-shifter or the classic werewolf. In Greek myth, a king named Lycaon tried to test Zeus's divinity by feeding him some children he killed for the purpose. When Zeus discovered this abomination, he punished Lycaon by turning him into a werewolf and putting all of his kinsmen to death.

Of course, the various versions of the story emphasize such things as male dominance, sexual development, and simple childhood warnings not to go where there is danger. It has been used for many purposes, as a good myth should. But the conflict between civilized human behavior and the hard facts of bloody nature remain in its bones.

Inciting Incident: The first meeting of the Wolf and Red and his proposal that he will help her through the forest. "Hello, little girl! Let me help you!" "Why, thank you, sir!"

Crisis: When Red enters the house and mistakes the Wolf for Grandma. "Oh Grandma, what big teeth you have," "All the better to eat you with, my dear."

Catastrophe: When the Wolf eats Red, "Yum, yum."

Climax: When the woodsman rescues Red and Grandma and kills the Wolf. "You have eaten these two beautiful women, and I will rescue them!" Bam goes the ax on the Wolf's head.

Denouement: "Thanks, Mr. Woodsman," "Why you are welcome, little missy!"

Notes

1 Longwell, Dennis and Meisner, Sanford. *Sanford Meisner on Acting*. 1st ed. New York: Vintage Original, 2004.
2 Csikszentmihalyi, Mihaly. *Applications of Flow in Human Development and Education: The Collected Works of Mihaly Csikszentmihalyi*. Dordrecht: Springer, 2014.
3 Kirk, Christine and Kirk, John. *On Directing*. New York: Xlibris, 2004.
4 This work was developed by John Kirk and Ralph Bellas in their book, *On Directing*, which even though it is not well known remains one of the most logical pieces of writing on the subject. It has been updated and reprinted, and I hope it will achieve the reputation it deserves.

Chapter 6

Two Hero's Journeys

The Hero's Journey of Muhammad Ali

Table 6.1 Muhammad Ali Journey

Innocent World of Childhood:	**Roots in Rebellion**
	Cassius Clay grew up in Louisville, Kentucky. He was born in 1942, and from all reports was a very sweet and well-behaved little boy. His father had troubles with alcohol and the home life was not particularly healthy.
	Cassius Clay was named after his father, who had been named for a white abolitionist. The abolitionist freed slaves and was finally murdered for his beliefs.
Magical Aid:	**Who Stole my Bike?**
	Twelve-year-old Cassius Clay tearfully asks policeman Joe Martin, *magical aid,* to help him find who stole his new red Schwinn bike.
	Cassius says he's "*gonna whup whoever stole it.*"
	Martin replies, "*Well, you better learn how to fight before you start challenging people that you're gonna whup.*"
	Martin runs a gym for youngsters to learn to box.
	With the policeman *Joe Martin* as Cassius's *first teacher and coach, he wins tournaments and championships.*
Call to Adventure:	**Islam**
	Cassius first hears about the Nation of Islam on a trip to Chicago for a *Golden Gloves Tournament.* He returns to Louisville with a vinyl record album of Elijah Muhammad's speeches.
	Notice the name of the *tournament*; it speaks of ancient things.

(Continued)

Table 6.1 (Continued)

At age 18, Cassius brings home a *gold medal* from the 1960 Rome *Olympics*. He throws the medal in the Ohio River as a private protest against racism.

Back in Louisville, he meets 6-year-old Lonnie Williams while sitting on the porch of his home. He will marry her in 1986. This is an example of what C.G. Jung calls, "synchronicity"; "the coincidental occurrence of events and especially psychic events (as similar thoughts in widely separated persons or a mental image of an unexpected event before it happens) that seem related but are not explained by conventional mechanisms of causality – used especially in the psychology of C. G. Jung" (*Merriam-Webster Dictionary*).

He starts his professional career, quickly gaining prominence. His braggadocio will delight and charm some, infuriate and repel others. This sort of behavior is very true of soldiers such as Achilles, et al.

Supernatural Aid, Angelo Dundee becomes his coach and trainer and stays with Ali throughout his boxing career.

Notice the synchronicity of the name Angelo. It is hard to write this stuff!

Refusal of the Call: **Not to Speak is to Speak**

Clay attends a Nation of Islam rally, but *does not speak publicly about his attraction to their message.*

His *father reveals that his son is a Muslim and speaks negatively about them to the press, after which he receives death threats.*

A Father who denies or in other ways rejects his son is a typical mythological trope.

Belly of the Whale: **Just Sit Tight.**

Clay starts to espouse principles of the Nation of Islam, but *does not announce his conversion.*

Crossing the Threshold: **Come Out and Fight!**

Malcolm X becomes a mentor, replacing the "dark father."

The night after he wins the Heavyweight Championship from Sonny Liston, a reporter asks Ali, "Are you a card-carrying member of the Black Muslims?" His reply, "*A rooster crows only when he sees the light. . . . I have seen the light, and I'm crowing.*"

He is given the new name of Muhammad Ali by Elijah Muhammad, leader of the Black Muslims. In renaming him, Elijah Muhammad becomes a new father. Thus Ali disavows not only his father but also the white man whose name he bears.

Of course, a figure as large as Ali speaks in poetry and allegory; it is his natural parlance.

Road of Trials:	**Betrayal by Friends**
	The old guard sportswriters and former friends turn on him and become *demons*, refusing to use his new Muslim name.
Tests and Ordeals:	**Damned If You Do and Damned If You Don't**
	Ali registers for the draft. Though he fails the mental aptitude tests and has been deemed unfit for service, nonetheless he receives a notice to report for army induction. He speaks out against the Vietnam War *and refuses to be inducted.*
	Draftees at the induction ceremony must step forward when their name is called. This ritual signifies acceptance of induction into the United States Armed Forces. Ali does not step forward.
More Tests and Ordeals:	**Conscientious Objector**
	Ali *claims exemption as a conscientious objector* and a minister of the Nation of Islam. His exemption is denied. It is probable that he knew what the outcome of this would be. His fight with racism has begun in earnest.
Dragon Battle	**The Viet Cong**
	Ali makes headlines across the country when he tells a reporter, "*I ain't got no quarrel with the Viet-Cong*"; this sets off a firestorm of criticism and anger. He becomes a pariah in the U.S. to many of his former fans.
Symbolic Death and Dismemberment:	**No Fights, No Rights, Stripped**
	Arrested and found guilty on draft evasion charges, Ali is stripped of his Heavyweight title, fined, and has his passport revoked. He stays out of jail on bond, but is banned from professional boxing in every state in the country. The country itself is enough of a jail.
Meeting the Goddess:	Because Ali can no longer be a fighter, he uses his other strength, the gift of speech, to connect with young people concerning the roots of the war and racism. He is very well received on college campuses.
	He marries Lonnie Williams in 1986. She is the little girl he met in his neighborhood when she was only 6 and had kept in touch with on and off for many years. She is his fourth wife. Lonnie is an MBA grad from UCLA and takes charge of Ali's mishmash of financial and legal affairs. Among other things she oversees building of a museum and education complex in Louisville, the Muhammad Ali Center.
Atonement with or Recognition by the Father:	Ali's father becomes a Muslim sometime in the late 1960s, thus recognizing his son and blessing him.

(Continued)

Table 6.1 (Continued)

Ultimate Boon:	Ali's boxing license is renewed. He returns to his boxing career and recaptures the Heavyweight title.
Apotheosis:	**Becoming Godlike**
	Ali retires from boxing having fulfilled that destiny. He is the most recognizable man in the world at this time.
Magic Flight and Crossing the Return Threshold:	**Olympian Honors**
	Ali lights the Olympic flame in the opening ceremonies of the 1996 Summer Olympic Games in Atlanta, Georgia. In doing so he crosses the return threshold, having reconciled not only with his family and friends, but also with the people of the U.S.
	How much myth do we need? *The Olympic Flame* was in honor of the *Titan God, Prometheus*, who was said to have created mankind and given fire to mortals. In one of the stories featuring Zeus's hatred of him, he is chained to a rock and has his liver pecked out daily. He is an interesting god to consider.
Master of the Two Worlds:	Ali retires and, as his Parkinson's disease worsens, the illness forces him to lose the reliance on his body and mind and to live within his soul.
Freedom to Live:	**Respect**
	In 2005, President George W. Bush presents Muhammad Ali with the Presidential Medal of Freedom.
	Ali's body failed him on June 3, 2016. The world mourned his loss. However, his irrepressible spirit no longer needs to fight for respect. He has completed his cycle on Earth brilliantly and now joins the stars and planets and the other gods in the stratosphere.

Hamlet's journey: A brief and debatable look at Hamlet as hero

In *Hamlet*, is Claudius actually a Father Figure for Hamlet? Is the play more Oedipal than it might appear to be? Does Polonius represent another face of the Father, foolish, but cagey? Is Laertes actually a brother figure? Or is Hamlet simply the Odyssey about a princely grad student? All of these concepts may change the structuring of the play and the actor's choice of archetype. The point of the search is to awaken the imagination, not to get it right. As Stanislavski says when quoting his teachers Schepkin and Schumsky (sorry, their names always makes me giggle because they sound like a vaudeville team), "It's not that you play well or badly, but that you play truly."

For the role of Hamlet, an actor might begin by examining avenging gods such as Orestes, who personifies both vengeance and madness; Horus, the Egyptian god who killed his usurping uncle, Seth; Jason of Argonaut fame and his uncle Pelias; Frodo Baggins; or anyone else whose energy is provoked by the need to vengeance and who fears taking it. The reason to find a true hero is that he or she will have many sides not limited to one quality. The most important element in this search is that the actor must somehow resonate with his or her choice. To repeat, archetypes differ from stereotypes in that they include *duality* as a necessary part of their being, as in C.J. Jung's concept of shadow and archetype or anima/animus. Jung discusses the idea that every human and therefore every archetype must contain within itself its own "shadow" or, as we might say, its opposite. Hamlet's *shadow* at the beginning of the show is a ruthless warrior, while his face to the world is an innocent scholar, a sort of eternal graduate student.

Another example is *A Streetcar Named Desire*. The rape scene between Stanley and Blanche may begin with Stanley as a Centaur and Blanche as the embodiment of Ishtar. Each of these archetypes implies unrepressed actions of one sort or another with very little psychology to weigh the actors down. Ishtar is both Good Mother and Monster Mother, and the Centaur is both gentle horse and rapacious stallion. As the archetype is determined, it is best for the actor to become an expert and to look at the archetype's journey. There will be many surprises in store.

Hamlet's Hero's Journey

Act I, scene I

The Ghost of Hamlet's father, *a supernatural guide*, is seen by the two guards on the castle's battlements; *the Call* is issued for Hamlet by the ghost even though Hamlet is not there.

Act I, scene 2

Hamlet, having crossed from England to Denmark from the *World of Innocence* to the new world of the marriage of Gertrude and Claudius, discovers how easily they have recovered from the death of his father. He loses his *Innocence* and is separated from his attenuated childhood in this scene. He is then *Called to Adventure* by Horatio and the guards as they tell of the vision of the Ghostly King and invite him to watch with them for the reappearance.

Act I, scene 4

At the castle's parapet, Hamlet's Father's Ghost, *The Supernatural Aid*, challenges Hamlet to avenge his murder; Hamlet *Accepts the Call* at this time. (This is the *Inciting Incident*.)

Act II, scene 2

Hamlet's next hero's step is to *Cross the Threshold*. He does so with his friends Rosenkranz and Guildenstern when Polonius acting as another *Magical Aid* brings in the players. It may be here where Hamlet descends into the *Belly of the Whale* and the players appear as *Helpers* to aid Hamlet to ensure that the Ghost is truly that of his father, in using the performance of the play to test the theory. Hamlet remains in the *Belly of the Whale* as he thrashes about in the "To be or not to be" soliloquy, not able to emerge as a hero yet. In order to do that he must die to his old self and sacrifice those things that tied him to that life. After the soliloquy, a *Temptress* enters in the body of Ophelia, and in disentangling himself from her he is enabled to set out on the *Road of Trials*.

Act III, scene 2

Hamlet reaches his bottom, his *sparagamos*, or *his abyss*,[1] as he symbolically dies and is reborn. He *takes leave of his old life* as prince/scholar and enters the new role as the canny and ruthless avenger that fate has decreed for him. The archetype that this implies is the merging of action with mind, not one-sided but multi-dimensional. His speech to the players is as much to himself about his own behavior as it is to them. Hamlet must be everything that he tells the players to do if he is to succeed. The players are a *challenge to action*.

Act III, scene 3

He comes upon the king at prayer and does nothing, a complete *Refusal of the Call*.

Act III, scene 4

Along this road of trials, buttressed by the *Supernatural Aid*, he *slays a dragon* when he kills Polonius, meets with the *Goddess, his Mother*, who represents both sides of the Goddess/Mother, and then uses *the murder of Gonzago* to test both his mother and the King.

Act IV, scene 3

Hamlet is sent back to England by Claudius, another *dragon or demon* setting a trap for him, supposedly to cover up the news of the murder. In fact, Claudius is plotting to have him killed while there.

Act IV, scene 4

Before leaving, Hamlet happens upon Fortinbras and his army. It seems that Hamlet is *being called again* to be the hero that Fortinbras already is, for Fortinbras has already avenged the death of his own father and is going to take the lands that belong to him. These are lands that were stolen by Hamlet's father in war. His impulsiveness is a foil for Hamlet's deliberative manner. He is a *Supernatural Aid* in this respect. Fortinbras has given him a prod to do his duty as Fortinbras has done his. This scene provokes Hamlet to *commit himself to action*, going from "How all occasions do inform against me" to "O, from this time forth/ My thoughts be bloody, or be nothing worth" in his final soliloquy. It is right and proper for heroes to take a vow.

Act V, scene I

In a *magical flight*, Hamlet returns after *crossing the mythical water* from the world of his studies to the chaos of Denmark. (In sending Hamlet back to England, Claudius can be seen as an *unwitting aid*). While on the ship (water implies secrets and rebirth here), Hamlet receives a *magical boon*; he discovers the letter from Claudius requesting that the king of England behead him. He craftily arranges that his former friends, *demons of a sort*, be killed for their betrayal. And with this foreknowledge he fights his way back through a *sea battle* and returns to Denmark *strengthened, reborn, and illuminated*. He has reached his *apotheosis*; he can come and go between worlds. His appearance at Ophelia's funeral is an opportunity to shock his uncle and the court. He jumps into the grave, which he no longer fears, and tussles with Laertes.

Act V, scene 2

Horatio reveals Hamlet's newly found strength, and Horatio becomes an *aid* to Hamlet in his revenge against Claudius. Osric, a *Fantastical Creature*, appears to *aid* Hamlet, telling him that Claudius's plot to kill him is known and that Laertes is going to challenge him to *a duel in the court*. (*This is the crisis.*)

After considering *refusing the call*, Hamlet *accepts his fate* and goes forth to the duel having *overcome his attachment to the world*. At this point, mortality to him is not an important matter.

> Not a whit, we defy augury.
> There's a special providence in the fall of a sparrow.
> If it be now, 'Tis not to come;
> if it be not to come, it will be now;
> if it be not now, yet it will come.
> The Readiness is all . . .

Act 5, scene 2

After little ado, Hamlet enters the *Final Battle* takes up the duel with Laertes and receives a wound from Laertes's poisoned sword. (*Structural Climax*)

> The point envenomed too! – Then, venom, to thy work.

Gertrude *the Mother Goddess attempts to rescue Hamlet* when she moves to wipe his brow and warns him not to drink. She drinks and dies for him. Hamlet then, already infected by the poison, kills Claudius, with both "envenom'd" sword and tainted wine. (*Climax*)

> Here, thou incestuous, murderous, damnèd Dane,
> Drink off this potion. Is thy union here?
> Follow my mother.

Hamlet's duty to his father is over; he can take *flight again;* he has moved past the desire for immortal physical life. His wish is to tell his story, but that is "not to be." (*Denouement*) embolden

O God, Horatio, what a wounded name,
Things standing thus unknown, shall live behind me!
If thou didst ever hold me in thy heart
Absent thee from felicity a while,
And in this harsh world draw thy breath in pain
To tell my story.

He has *Atoned with his Father* in this revenge; he now belongs to Heaven, where hopefully his atonement will release his father from wandering as a ghost, and Horatio will make sure that he is not damned by those who don't know his fated story. In essence he has suffered and died to clear the court and the land of the evils that infect it. He has become *Master of Two Worlds*. However his legacy will not be in this world. He will not become a king; he will instead take up residence "forever in the blessed isle of the un-aging Goddess of Immortal Being," as Campbell puts it.[2]

Even with *Hamlet*, or maybe especially with *Hamlet*, there will be disagreement both as to the structural and Hero's Journey analyses; it is in the rehearsal where such things must be finally tested by the director and the players. Certainly my rendition of this story is only one way of telling it. Debate at this point is good to define the structure of the play for each of the participants including the director or teacher (none of whom will ever be 100 percent right when it comes to a great play). And not all elements of the Hero's Journey are going to be in each story.

Notes

1 In *The Hero With a Thousand Faces* (2nd Ed. Bollingen Series XVII). Princeton, NJ: Princeton, University Press, 1968. Joseph Campbell refers to this stage as the "Sparagamos," which means tearing apart in Greek and is meant to symbolize a ritual death of the Hero in other settings.
2 Campbell, *Thousand Faces*, 167.

Chapter 7

Bridging and Superscenes

Bridges

In order to clarify the use of archetype, consider an actor who has chosen the goddess "Diana." This goddess was a celibate huntress, revered for her ability to assist women in childbirth. If she is chosen as the archetype, the actor in question would do gestures and corporeal movements involving hunting, catching, and slaughtering, as well as assisting in birth. Diana is an archetype, as opposed to a stereotype, because she contains opposing energies, in this case, birth versus slaughter.

Ingredients

A large space with mats for movement
Barefoot actors

Instructions

1 Have the cast begin moving on the mats, using the grid at varying tempos and all other elements of Viewpointing. Once the students are able to achieve soft focus and seem to be settled into the sort of concentration that VPs provide, ask them to stop and position themselves with enough space around them to gesture and move without interfering with other actors.

2 After this is established, instruct the actors that every time you clap your hands they should move in place with a gesture or positional change. Ask them to hold the position until the next handclap. Do this three times and then repeat the gestures/movements. An example might be clap #1, touching the nose; clap #2 falling to the floor; clap #3 kneeling

with hands outreached. Then ask for a new sequence of three different moves, again done with three claps.

3   The claps can be evenly spaced or random until you observe that the participants are not planning what they will do next. Do this in sequences of three claps each time. Allow just about anything except planning or literal sports or dance movements.

4   Once the actors have repeated this several times, clap, ask them to hold, and request that they redo the last tripartite sequence by making it as large as possible, then as small as possible, then as fast, and then as slowly. They should be instructed to examine the beginning, the middle, and the end of the movement, making sure that the energy remains constant. You also may say, "Do this only with your foot, your butt, your knee," or any other part of their corpus.

5   As they become adept at this assignment, ask the actors to simply think about the archetypes they have chosen and the essential actions attached to them. I sometimes ask, "What are the physical tools presented to you by whichever hero you have chosen to use? For instance, Hercules's strength and aggression, or Diana's hunting ability and her magical power to control animals."

6   Again with the three claps, suggest that they do a gesture or movement using the tools of the god they are investigating. There should be a quick flow through this series of movements to avoid both literalness and intellectual choice; let the actors play with speed, impulse, and shape using earlier instructions.

7   Once this has been accomplished three times, ask them to choose one of the triple and repeat it slowly. Suggest that they do this by using extremities of rhythm and speed. You may want to call out "extremely fast" and then surprise them with "medium," "extremely large," or "too small to be seen."

8   You can suggest that the participants do the beginning of the movement, #1, extremely fast and extremely large; then the middle, #2, at medium speed and medium small; and the final stroke, #3, at extremely slow and medium size. The point is to mix it up until the actors themselves begin to experiment with these elements.

9   Ask the actors now to remain stationary as you shout out the numbers, 1, 2, 3. The actors should fully express the sequence they have chosen for themselves using whatever instruction of size or speed they desire. The rhythm of the calls can be random or even.

10 Once the actors have completed this, ask them to stand opposite a partner. As you call out numbers (1, 2, 3), have the two perform the individual parts of their sequences in opposition to each other. So partner A will do the first part of the gesture, #1 (touching her nose), at partner B, then partner B will do the first part of his or her gesture, #1 (stomping on the floor), at partner A, and both will move to fulfill all three sections in like manner.

Suggestion

The actor teams *should not try to relate*, they should be told to *simply observe and send*. Each actor should maintain personal distance with no physical touching, never going to full rest. They will want to be responsive to each other, but stifle the urges until they become really necessary. After repeating their three expressions in opposition to one another several times so that they know the "dance," ask each participant to step out of the duet go back to their original space and to come up with gestures which are the exact opposites of the original ones (for example, instead of touching a nose with one hand, slap a knee with one foot). If their original gesture was gentle and caressing, the opposite one should be aggressive and assertive. All should once again shape the gesture into thirds and play with speed and size. Actors who have worked with Rudolph Laban's ideas of effort and quality in movement[1] are usually pretty good at this, and if you have time, you might want to discuss those principles.

11 These new antithetical gestures will now be called 1A, 2A, and 3A. Move back into pairs, and while maintaining connection to the partner, as the instructor calls out the numbers, have the actors perform each of their new antithetical gestures (1A, 2A, and 3A) at each other in the same way as before.

12 Once the partners fully understand their three primary and three antithetical gestures, begin varying the numbers being called out (example: 1, 2A, 3, 2, 3A, 1A . . . etc.). Example: partner A slaps her knee aggressively with her opposing foot; partner B, who had stomped on the floor aggressively, might reach for the sky longingly.

13 You may wish to ask them to trade gestures, letting Hercules do Diana's dance and Diana that of Hercules. This is a good test of focus and clarity for both actors.

14 Finally, allow the actors to respond fully together and acknowledge their instincts to respond to their partners and to create a sort of narrative. Discourage too much talk and too much creativity. The object is to rely on physical action alone to do most of the work through speed and shape.

15 Let each team perform their movement/drama for the rest of the class. This can encourage respect and understanding in the group and can further expand the ability of the ensemble to come together. It also underlines the concept that we are always seeking narrative because one will make itself known without being defined.

Discussion

- How did you feel doing the gesture at your partner but not for your partner?
- What was the story you were telling yourself about your partner?
- In terms of storytelling, what do you now realize that you didn't before we did this exercise?
- Did the story change when you were allowed to be in relationship?
- How did the reciprocal exchange of actions affect your actions?
- How is an action different from a gesture?

Superscenes

Superscenes are exercises in which actors physically explore the archetypal conflicts in the essential relationships of the text in a fully physical way. They begin without words. Their aim is to move past personality and into biology and impulse as motivating forces. They are meant to unearth the hidden complexities of original conflicts. When observed, they look like a cross between a dance and a wrestling match. The primacy of physical action is a way of reinforcing the understanding that language is a less risky and socialized form for the communication of primal needs. Ultimately, a hoped-for reconnection between the physical and the verbal will be attained. For video demonstrations, go to http://www.janedrakebrody.com.

Purpose of Superscenes

Superscenes move past an actor's idiosyncratic patterns of behavior and his or her intellectual decisions. They move from an archetypal base to allow raw physical impulse to lead, as prompted by physical response to the acting partner's actions.

Ingredients

A large enough space for unrestricted movement
Wrestling mats
Barefoot actors

Instructions

1 Actors begin the scenes on wrestling mats, without words, slowly walking across from each other clockwise on the edge of the mats with "soft eyes." Once this level of concentration can be observed, they can begin to watch each other objectively until one or the other of them feels ready to make an assertive move. During this stalking and seeking behavior, no social interaction is allowed until one or the other of the actors decides to aggress or interfere with his opposite. The director/teacher must be careful to allow this to play out; it can take a while, and rushing only makes the actors self-conscious. Actors may feel the need to move before they are ready because they want to be good team members. If that occurs, the coach must ask the two to return to stalking or seeking until one or the other of them actually want to aggress. I usually suggest meditating on the god or hero they have chosen as they walk and envision being infected in their gut by that god.

2 Finally, one partner will aggress; perhaps the woman playing Ishtar throws herself into the Centaur's arms, and the actor playing the Centaur attempts to conquer the wild Ishtar. Full bodily contact is necessary, and noncorporeal gesture is discouraged as communication. In the case of Sam Shepard's *A Lie of the Mind*, the actors playing Jake and his mother, Lorraine, meet on the mat; Lorraine might use the concept of the Assyrian monster mother Tiamat, and Jake, the Greek demigod Narcissus. The physical manifestation may begin with the Lorraine/Tiamat, the mother attempting to rock the child, and if that is the most powerful urge between the two of them, Jake/Narcissus must fully allow himself to be rocked until one or the other of them releases from the hold. It is important for the actors to feel that something is completed before moving forward.

3 Using the idea Push/Pull/Hold/Release, the actors are encouraged to physically express all their impulses of whatever kind. They are instructed to stop and hold when the impulse to do so is felt between them, locking eyes. As the two hold, they observe and interpret whatever nonverbal signals they are receiving.

Following this assessment, they must release away from each other and return to physical conflict predicated upon the information gleaned from the "hold." Be careful that the release not be a rest unless it is a total "give up movement" such as lying down in a fetal position.

4 During an embrace, the two actors may stop all movement for a moment, contact each other visually, and then release to another conflict, depending on the impulse, just as in kinesthetic response in Viewpoints. For the director or coach, the aim is to speak as little as possible; not to direct, simply to encourage fulfillment of actions and communication. I frequently say such things as, "Finish it," "Know when you are done," and "Go all the way with that."

The actors must be made aware that conflict must always be pursued. After the opening actions, i.e., rocking and taming, the two move impulsively from protective ideas to murderous impulses to sexual feelings and so forth. The only rule is that the conflict may never end, although it will ebb and flow as the actors engage using holds and releases.

It is the job of the coach to end the scene, not the actors. Frequently, the actors may decide to end the piece just at the moment it is about to expand. The coach must push the actors past this moment until he or she feels that the work is actually finished on the scene. Such scenes can last between five and fifteen minutes. As with Grotowski's work, exhaustion plays its part.[2]

5 As this contact grows, the actors acknowledge wins and losses through tactical changes. The actors are side-coached by the teacher or director to seek conflict and to accept changes in speed, rhythm, intensity, fatigue, need, and desire to stop. A good phrase to use is "explore that further." However, my aim is always to have the actors finally increase their own skill to the point where I have no need to speak except to say "Yes" or "Go!"

Depending on the scene and play, I will prompt other members of the cast or class to join the scene even though they may not officially appear in it. For instance, in *Measure for Measure*, Claudio may be asked to join the Superscene as an equal participant with Isabella and Angelo. In *A Lie of the Mind*, another actor may enter to play the absent father with the mother/son duo. Sometimes, half the class may be positioned on the mat as a family: Jake, Lorraine, Frankie, the sister, and the father, all ready to enter the fray or exit it as they desire.

6 I may decide to enlist an actor from the sidelines to play "Death" or another such active element in the scene. It is useful when the important elements of the play are "othered" and personalized using Declan Donnellan's ideas about Juliet's balcony.[3] Concepts without faces are not as strong as fully embodied "gods" such as Death, Lust, Rage, and so on. In Shakespeare's day they knew this, and when he (or his devotees) capitalized words containing such large ideas, it gave them a palpable substance denied to lower-case items.

7 Important props and furniture can also be personified. For instance, in *Angels in America, Perestroika pt. 2*, the radio that connects the angels to the world's happenings is losing its power. The emotional connection to the radio and the stakes in the scene can be raised if the radio is personified by an actor who takes part in the scene as a dying soothsayer instead of a mechanical radio. This enables the actors attempting to revive it to fully appreciate its value.

8 I may ask the observing ensemble members to take notes of the actors' "map" and poses, or recently I have been videoing the scenes, an aid in mapping the work. These physical maps/moments/poses will be built upon as the scene is investigated further. When an important moment is discovered, I will sometimes call "Hold" so that the information can be transcribed in some way. We do not stop to discuss the pose, and as soon as possible the actors are prompted to release and continue. It is essential that some poses, movements, spatial relationships, or other elements created in the Superscene be kept in whatever form for use in the performance. This will be the "blocking" or "staging," with some adjustments for technical issues.

These staging guideposts support the actors' muscle memory as well as their awareness of the "dance" that the two of them (or more) have created. The retention may seem to be as realistic as sitting at a desk and kicking one's legs, where in the Superscene the legs had been kicking to escape from a partner who was trying to arrest the other's ability to move; or it may be as symbolic as lying on the floor kicking like a baby against a partner's verbal communication, or maybe the kick turns into jabbing with a finger or bumping with a hip. The vital piece of this is the action of kicking and its implication in the relationship at the time of the original Superscene. Obviously, the actor can kick with his words, but maintaining a degree of the physical map of the scene will keep the spontaneity and excitement of the scene alive more fully. The 'dance' can serve as a great warm up for the actors, or as a refresher if the scene gets stale in performance.

9   When the scene approaches physical exhaustion and depending on the actors' progress in responding impulsively, the participants may be prompted to "blurt" whatever sounds they seem to be repressing during the strenuous activity. These sounds are repeated and generally aid in the physical expression of the action. Blurts are not words or phrases; they are the oofs and uhhs that frequently accompany physical exertion. The actors must resist the desire to move into narrative. If the coach senses that blurts are being withheld, he or she must encourage the actor to release the built-up stress with sound. I don't always do this exercise unless I see the need in the actors to express verbally. Making these primitive sounds also can connect the actor to a voice he or she may not realize exists in their body. There have been occasions where I give the actors the words "yes" and "no" to use instead of blurts. Sometimes I may use "No, it's mine" or "No you will not" as phrases, depending on the actors and the scenes.

10   The next big step is a very delicate point wherein the director, teacher, fellow cast member, or assistant director slowly feeds the actors the lines (in phrases only, not complete speeches) from the scene. *It is vital that the actors be prompted not to interpret the meaning of the lines except as indicated by the physical effort occurring in the scene in the moment.* If they do so, stop and redo until the line takes its meaning from the interchange and cannot stand on its own. For instance, the line may be, "You stole my watch," but the two actors may be embracing. If so, the line may mean something like "I can't let go" or "I have trapped you" or "You have defeated me" or whatever is going on physically. This is an extremely important step because it enables the actors to get out of their heads, to let go of literalism, and *allows the subtext to rule.* This can be done even if the actors have already memorized the script. Either way, the physical dance/conflict must be retained with little regard for the literal meaning of the language. *It is the distance between the text and the subtext that is most intriguing to us.*

If the actors back away from full physicalization upon this introduction of language, they are instructed to drop the words and return to sounds or silence; whichever feels more comfortable. Once they seem ready to receive the language again, the lines must be dropped in *at the peak* of an interchange, not in a hold or a release initially. The actor's tendency will be to stop moving and to stand and interpret the lines; this must be discouraged. Eventually, they will be allowed to eliminate overt movement, but not at this point in the exercise.

11 As soon as the actors are fully engaged, whether with language or not, the director/teacher may decide to explore various adjustments toward working with the scene while maintaining the depth of the relationship and action in the scene. The first adjustment that I give for the actors who seem ready to move ahead is to immediately move into the "rehearsal set" we have agreed upon. For instance, in *Angels in America*, Roy Cohn's room needs only a bed, a bedside table, and a chair, even though in performance it will contain other things. This must be done quietly and quickly. Let ensemble members help with this. As soon as the scene is set, the actors do the scene with lines, either dropped in or memorized or a combination of the two, maintaining as much of the physical score of the Superscene as possible. Of course, owing to obstacles on the set or restriction of movement caused by it, there will probably be a less physical score. In speaking of Roy Cohn's bed, let me reiterate that this enormously important piece of furniture must be alive for Roy; it will morph from being a place of rest and refuge, to a jail, to a mother, to a place of torture, and so on. I make sure that in rehearsals we spend some time having actors personify the important scenic elements in a scene.

Once again, characters and ideas discussed in the scene may be asked to join the scene on the set and to improv, keeping the stakes very high and the physical conflict alive. In the case of *Lie of the Mind*, the Father is almost always metaphorically present for Jake and his family. A member of the ensemble would therefore work in the scene as the living father and have physical contact with Jake and Lorraine. There are many, many variations on this move from Superscene to textual scene, but the most vital aspect is that when the actors do so, the physical exploration must be honored as the truth beneath the situation. For instance, Jake's Father could be in bed with him while Lorraine attempts to feed them both.

Generally, the scene is ready to be performed at this time, the lines should be fairly well learned, and the actors will have a sense of the map of the scene and how they can play within it. If special staging is needed for lights or other technical aspects, we work that into the staging map.

Superscenes and memory

There is a great deal of neuroscience concerning memory and the need for sleep in relation to retention of ideas, images, and text. This will be discussed in Chapter 8. Briefly however, Superscene work is an enormous aid to memory because it keeps the actor from seeing the lines on the page in front of his or her eyes from the beginning of the process. The lines will be implanted in the muscle memory and in the amygdala, where they are more easily retained and recalled. The process for this is as follows:

1   Once the lines have been dropped into a Superscene, the actors are asked to wait an hour or two and then spend about fifteen minutes, no more, silently reading them alone without interpretation and walking if possible.

2   They are instructed that after that they should forget about the scene and go on with their daily activities. They must allow at least six hours to elapse before reading or working on the scene again. Optimally, this will be an over-night sleep or at least a nap. Upon awakening, they read the scene again and realize how well they know it. Prior to starting the next rehearsal, the actors walk around the space together retracing occurrences in the Superscenes, quietly saying the lines without interpretation while someone from the cast or the assistant director helps when they need to call for a line.

3   For the director as well as for the actor, it is important to notice what isn't memorized because the missing issue, word, image, line, may lead to another Superscene or improvisation and may reveal some new ideas. No pressure should be attached to this lack of memory. The Superscene that ensues should be structured in such a way as to Concretize the absent concept. The basis of this idea is that the actor must never feel pressured to do anything as a corrective.

Notes

1 Hodgson, John. *Mastering Movement; The Life and Work of Rudolf Laban.* New York: Routledge, 2001.
2 Richards, Thomas. *At Work with Grotowski on Physical Actions.* London: Routledge, 1993.
3 Donnellan, Declan. *The Actor and the Target.* London: Nick Hern Books, 2005.

Part III

Neuroscience and images

Chapter 8

Mirror neurons, emotions, memory, meditation, embodiment, and images

The limbic system

I have always been annoyed by the subjectivity of my profession and by the belief of many that this is a natural state of affairs. The art of acting, teaching, and/or directing has been without scrutiny, to the point that most practitioners will ultimately say, "Whatever works." And yet, the greatest teacher of them all, Konstantin Stanislavski, was forever seeking a logical system for actors to use.

The rationale for writing this chapter is my own desire to find at least a modicum of objective proof for acting pedagogy. As a long-time acting teacher, I feel a responsibility to give actors something more than my anecdotal experience. In the future, we should be able to move toward a measureable and scientific way of teaching. This would require establishing control groups and populations as well as doing experiments with equipment not available to most of us at this time. Indeed, if we were able to secure the use of an fMRI machine, the sort of equipment currently in use forces the subject to be still and alone. Even when attempting to overcome this problem through virtual hook-ups to videos and so forth, no instrument of measurement currently exists to study brain behavior during human physical interchanges with the amount of specificity necessary. As with all technology, we can look forward to the day when technical advances produce wearable fMRI "hats" of some kind, but until then we must be content to study responses that are at some remove from the active body. It is my hope for the future, when the technical problems are solved, that there will be those who study the scientific aspects of acting theory using some great hats!

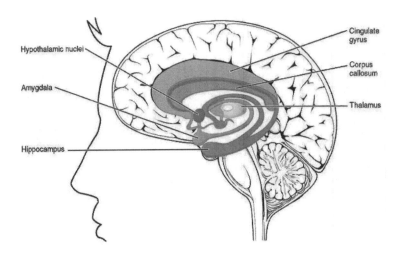

Figure 8.1 The limbic system

Illustration from Anatomy & Physiology, Connexions web site: http://cnx.org/content/col11496/1.6, June 19, 2013.

Over the past twelve years, I have explored the subject matter relating to action, emotion, and memory in scientific articles and books and then tested the hypotheses suggested by them through creating exercises both for classrooms and rehearsals. My only means of evaluation of their efficacy has been the response from actors and directors whose work has been changed by their use and by the response of audiences who sense something unusual going on. Unfortunately, once again, this is subjective. Not subjective, however, are the theories upon which I base the exercises.

The eternally balancing body

All of the exercises in this book, both mine and others, are based on a rather simple premise. That premise is that everything that happens in the body/mind and every action taken toward the world occurs to ensure the health and abundant survival of the organism. The sensory responses – seeing, hearing, touching, smelling, and tasting – exist to maintain balance in the body. We are automatically programmed to monitor ourselves in the same way that my new refrigerator attempts to maintain a constant temperature and humidity level.

Antonio Damasio, famed neurologist and scholar, describes it thusly:

> All living organisms from the humble amoeba to the human are born with devices designed to solve automatically, no proper reasoning required, the basic problems of life. Those problems are finding sources of energy; incorporating and transforming energy; maintaining a chemical balance of the interior compatible with the life process; maintaining the organism's structure by repairing its wear and tear; and fending off external agents of disease and physical injury. The single word *homeostasis* is convenient shorthand for the ensemble of regulations and the resulting state of regulated life.[1]

This phenomenon is not limited to humans; it is the way of every living thing including the earth itself. The same self-regulation goes on in a worm, in a toad, in a weasel, in a man, in a family, in a community, in a society, in a country, in a continent, and finally in the ecosphere. All organic things seek to maximize pleasure and growth and minimize pain and injury and, therefore, must eliminate obstacles to that survival.

In order to do so, there must first be a biological excitation in the body experienced through the senses as threat or pleasure. This response is a chemical and electrical one that we call "emotion." The methods of maintaining balance are ecologically determined.

Emotion is elicited below our consciousness through all of the five senses in the primal brain. The body readies for action almost simultaneously, and after this is already in motion, the human experiences "feelings." One might think of "emotion" as the underlying biological response that is too large to be dealt with. This idea means that "feelings" are never all of the biology, only those which are interpreted by the body in a narrower sense.

Feelings are a result of these cruder emotions and are named and justified by the higher brain to be either acted upon or rejected. In other words, our responses to the world happen before we know it, and we then justify our actions logically. Before rationality, the body is engaged.

> Fear feelings and pounding hearts are both effects caused by the activity of this [emotional] system which does the job unconsciously, literally, before we actually know we are in danger.

The system that detects danger is the fundamental mechanism of *fear*, and the behavioral, physiological, and conscious manifestations are the surface responses it orchestrates.[2]

Emotion is acted upon depending upon the circumstance in which it occurs and the history of the object or person involved. For instance, when we are surprised, *our emotion (the fear of attack)* will be engaged. However, *what we do* about the surprise, and how much credence we give to the *feeling aroused*, is not at all predictable. If a clown jumps out of a box at a birthday party, after the initial startle (emotion of fear), most of us will be in some way amused (amusement) or annoyed (annoyance) depending on one's prior experience of clowns. The imbalance of such a surprise will generally be offset by laughter.[3]

However if the same clown should jump out of a box in front of your bedroom window at night, after the initial startle, you may feel terror and take action to restore your peaceful homeostasis by running away or getting a butcher knife or pulling down the shade and calling the police. The larger the threat, the more action needed to regain equilibrium.

Summation

We have emotions to signal the body to prepare for action in order to reestablish balance. The emotions themselves are not perceived consciously, nor can they be controlled or accessed consciously, until they attain the status of feelings that are circumstantial. Emotions and their regulation are the background music of our existence, keeping the rhythm of everyday life stable. It is this stability that is sought by every organism. As Goldilocks says while seeking comfort for the night: "This one is too hard, and this one is too soft, but this one is just right!"

Meditation

As we are aware, the ancient practice of meditation exists across cultures as a means to quiet the noisy brain, to pray, to think deeply, and to heal an anxious soul. It is a *balancing* mechanism. Meditation in this case means paying attention to breath and the mind to achieve peace within.

My reason for encouraging as much mindful meditation as possible for actors is based in the observation that meditation slows the ceaselessly restless brain and teaches it to quietly focus rather than wander like a lost child seeking its mother. The ability to create a center of calm is vital to actors because the experience of being on stage creates a chemical response in the actor's corpus that is translated into panic, or self-consciousness, and much static in the mind. Many actors lose their breath, go "weak in the knees," forget everything they ever learned, or are unable to speak or see clearly in this sort of panic. (As a young performer, I literally vomited on my auditors, who were just too close for comfort). If the actor has attuned his or her body to calmness with breath, this reaction can be minimized, and if the actor is instead busy doing actions, the feeling of being watched, or stalked, or judged can be ameliorated.

The inability to find a calm center is probably the cause of most acting, movement, and vocal problems because the body's response to fear is to shut down those elements of behavior that the actor desperately needs. When everything in one's body is saying "red alert," the denial of the emotion causes further attempts by the instrument (body) to warn the actor about the danger of staying where he or she happens to be. It is telling her to freeze at first then to run or hide, or, at last gasp, to fight. The adrenalin is not an aid to memory or feeling or language processing.

Practiced meditators learn to be in the "moment" and to let it pass without judgment of its quality. They allow the world to happen, and, owing to the techniques of breathing and attention, the body isn't overly aroused. Actors need to do exactly that – to accept each moment as it arises and respond as needed. Alcoholics Anonymous has a phrase that I use frequently when actors are stuck or panicked:

Acceptance is the answer to ALL of my problems today. When I am disturbed, it is because I find some person, place, thing or situation – some fact of my life – unacceptable to me, and I can find no serenity until I accept that person, place, thing.[4]

Those who are true meditators condition themselves to avoid the destructive self-centeredness stemming from fear that plagues many actors. Self-centeredness is based in shame, in the potential discovery of flaws or weakness, and it forces the mind to be constantly on guard for such revelations. When an actor experiences this, he or she is not actually in the scene. The scene they *are* in is attempting to cover the shameful exposure of their inadequate selves, and in the grip of this "seizure" they are incapable of receiving the help they so badly need from the environment or the partner to return to the living!

Experienced meditators of whatever school are trained to identify this sort of self-involvement uncritically and to release harmful feelings and thoughts through their practice. They strive to be fully in the "now," not in the future or in the past. Meditation enables its devotees to find calm and detachment, thus freeing the mind of obstacles to action in times of difficulty. This ability is a result of measurable physical changes in the brain produced through mindful meditation. It is this quality of acceptance of the present that allows for a peaceful journey through the world. The brilliant director and theatre theorist Declan Donnellan, in his book *The Actor and the Target*, makes the observation that "Fear governs the future as Anxiety, and the past as Guilt. . . . Fear cannot breathe while the actor remains [in the] present."[5]

Sharon Carnicke[6] confirms that Hatha Yoga was fundamental to Stanislavski's development of the System, but that American practitioners as well as academics ignored it. Soviet repression certainly influenced its absence from the books published at the time.

While there have been many studies, I am choosing to illustrate this with an fMRI study lead by Dr Judson Brewer at Yale University in 2011. Ten years prior to the study, Brewer had, as a medical student, learned to overcome the stress of medical school by learning to meditate, a practice he maintains to this day. The experiment was designed to determine if there were differences in the brains of meditators on a neuronal level. He chose a group of twelve experienced meditators (EMs) and a group of twelve non-meditators (NMs) as controls on the experiment.[7]

Non-meditators, when asked to sit quietly, allow their minds to wander. Especially in times of stress, the wandering brain tends to look for danger and difficulty as a means of preparing to combat them. The brain is constantly moving and searching, rarely stopping its relentless activity. This can be observed through fMRI imaging. The restlessness activates a portion of the brain called the DMN or default-mode network. Brewer states: "This network has been associated with processes ranging from attentional lapses to anxiety to clinical disorders, such as attention-deficit hyperactivity disorder (ADHD) and Alzheimer's disease."

In the experiment, all participants, both EMs and NMs, reported that they were able to follow the three different meditation cues quoted below. I include them not only as explanation but also as cues for those leading meditation in class or rehearsal. Any of these can be done alone or with other cues:

> *Concentration:* The object of which is to reduce mind wandering and its associated stress through an emphasis on breath awareness.
>
>> Cue: Please pay attention to the physical sensation of the breath wherever you feel it most strongly in the body. Follow the natural and spontaneous movement of the breath, not trying to change it in any way. Just pay attention to it. If you find that your attention has wandered to something else, gently but firmly bring it back to the physical sensation of the breath.
>
> *Loving-Kindness:* This meditation is based in altruistic thoughts for the health and happiness of yourself and others.
>
>> Cue: Please think of a time when you genuinely wished someone well (pause). Using this feeling as a focus, silently wish all beings well, by repeating a few short phrases of your choosing over and over. For example: May all beings be happy, may all beings be healthy, may all beings be safe from harm.
>
> *Choice-less Awareness:* Directly attending to whatever arises in one's conscious field of awareness at any moment and accepting it without holding onto it mentally. (This means releasing the thought from your consciousness if a new thought enters rather than attempting to hold onto the original one.)
>
>> Cue: Please pay attention to whatever comes into your awareness, whether it is a thought, emotion, or body sensation. Just follow it until something else comes into your awareness, not trying to hold onto it or change it in any way. When something else comes into your awareness, just pay attention to it until the next thing comes along.

The fMRI administered following the cues revealed definite differences the brains of the two groups before and after the experiment was begun. Further, it showed that after the experiment, the

EMs demonstrated that differing cues changed their brains only in correspondingly different areas. In contrast, the brains of the NMs were activated in the harmful default mode network (DMN).

We found that the main nodes of the default-mode network [DMN] (medial prefrontal and posterior cingulate cortices) were relatively deactivated in experienced meditators across all meditation types. Furthermore, functional connectivity analysis revealed stronger coupling in experienced meditators between the posterior cingulate, dorsal anterior cingulate, and dorsolateral prefrontal cortices (regions previously implicated in self-monitoring and cognitive control), both at baseline and during meditation. Our findings demonstrate differences in the default-mode network that are consistent with decreased mind wandering. As such, these provide a unique understanding of possible neural mechanisms of meditation.[8]

There are critics of meditation studies for various reasons having to do with the efficacy of the methods used as well as possible overemphasis of the subject matter because of its popularity. However, most practitioners and observers will confirm that the 2011 findings seem to reflect their experiences. As a theatre person and long-time actor trainer, I can attest that actors who use meditation as a foundation are far happier, more flexible, more open to creativity, and easier to work with than those whose default position is a wandering mind and fearful anxiety.

The phenomenologist, philosopher, skeptic, cognitive scientist, biologist, and critic Daniel C. Dennett says the following:

Francisco Varela, an immunologist-turned-neuroscientist, Evan Thompson, a philosopher, and Eleanor Rosch, a psychologist, are radical critics of cognitive science. . . . They have pooled their skills to execute what is surely the best informed, best balanced radical critique to date. Just how radical? Their heroes are the Buddha and the French phenomenologist, Maurice Merleau-Ponty. They argue that Buddhist meditative traditions offer not just a wealth of important phenomena of human consciousness, but otherwise unobtainable insights into the relations of embodiment that permit us to understand how the inner and the outer, the first-person point of view and the objective point of view of science, can coexist.[9]

Summation

If intention becomes action through an enlistment of the body/ brain using sensory signals, then pulling that duo together through meditation should make intention/action powerful and clear. If, however, the actor has not been able to heal this Cartesian split, his or her actions may be muddled and underperformed.

Phenomenology: The study of the experience of intention

The Stanford Encyclopedia of Philosophy states,

> Phenomenology is the study of structures of consciousness as experienced from the first-person point of view. The central structure of an experience is its intentionality, its being directed *toward* something. It is an experience of or about some person (or object). An experience is directed toward an object (or person) by virtue of its content or meaning (which represents the object) together with appropriate enabling conditions.[10]

In other words, I know I exist by what I do and how I feel, by directing my action towards something outside of me that has a meaning to me in an appropriate manner. I live in the world of my senses and interpret it using them. I live my life every day and deal with things from my own perspective as they arise.[11]

I include this brief section on phenomenology because I believe it is a vital study for directors and acting teachers. If in our various capacities we are working with normal biological beings, it seems only obvious that we should learn at least a bit about how they function. The phenomenological point of view seems particularly appropriate because it is at once a philosophical and a practical means of understanding how humans work.

The classic book *The Embodied Mind*, written by Evan Thompson, Eleanor Rosch, and the late Francisco Varela, challenged the popular general view, espoused by cognitive science at that time (1992), that the workings of the brain were more or less like a computer.[12]

On my first reading of *The Embodied Mind*, I was taken by the statement:

> We propose as a name, the term *enactive* to emphasize the growing conviction that cognition is not the representation of a

pregiven world by a pregiven mind but is rather the *enactment* of a world and a mind on the *basis of a history of the variety of actions* that a being in the world performs.

(Author's emphasis)

The emphasis on action rather than programming as the means of finding both meaning and self in the world appealed to my growing conviction that acting must be based on *action and interaction* rather than a "pregiven mind." As well, the definition of "embodied" used in the title signifies "reflection in which the body and mind have been brought together." This clarified for me the necessity for actors to "get out of their heads," a phrase that I, and other teachers and directors, have used frequently. The "embodied or enactive" idea removes the image of a somehow disconnected "head" from which one must somehow detach one's self and puts in its place the vision of a head and body that remain connected. Embodiment releases the mind/body to do its thing. Finally, the mention of "a history of a variety of actions" comes close to the idea of given circumstances.

The cognitive scientist Daniel C. Dennett, in the article quoted earlier, goes on to say:

The basic intentional structure of consciousness, we find in reflection or analysis, involves further forms of experience. Thus, phenomenology develops a complex account of temporal awareness (within the stream of consciousness), spatial awareness (notably in perception), attention (distinguishing focal and marginal or "horizontal" awareness), awareness of one's own experience (self-consciousness, in one sense), self-awareness (awareness-of-oneself), the self in different roles (as thinking, acting, etc.), embodied action (including kinesthetic awareness of one's movement), purpose or intention in action (more or less explicit), awareness of other persons (in empathy, intersubjectivity, collectivity), linguistic activity (involving meaning, communication, understanding others), social interaction (including collective action), and everyday activity in our surrounding life-world (in a particular culture).[13] This long list, when taken apart, describes the essence of the study of acting. It almost recreates the chart brought to the United States by Stella Adler after working with Stanislavski and copied by Bobby Lewis, also a well-known actor and acting teacher at the time. All of its components are engaged when doing any of the exercises described in the experiential area of this book. The Stanislavski Chart is in the appendix to this chapter.

I am using my own language here to assist in linking it to practice.

Temporal awareness: Time and rhythm.

Spatial awareness: Positioning in relationship to space, size, and high/low. The understanding that geography is destiny.

Attention: Being conscious of surroundings both near and far.

Awareness of one's own experience: Being aware of the accumulation of action over time as well as the moment at hand.

Self-awareness: Being attuned to one's actions.

Self in different roles: Being able to switch between modes of behavior.

Embodied action: Movement and action joined in the body.

Purpose or intention of action: Awareness of motive.

Linguistic activity: Listening and speaking, taking "turns."

Social interaction: Flexibility in moving from single to partner to others and behaving appropriately within the given limitations of the purpose of the interaction.

Everyday activity in a particular culture: Awareness and ability to execute mores and manners.

Summation

We train actors in awareness through such methods as Improvisation, Alexander, Fitzmaurice, Meisner, Viewpoints, Laban, and others. The point of most of these methods is the same as the point of meditation: To free the actor of self-consciousness physically, intellectually, and emotionally. Meditation awakens awareness and frees the actor's soul. For actors, the multiple layers of awareness attended to by phenomenology as well as the findings concerning the use of meditation are all important elements of teaching and directing in the theatre.

Mirror neurons

A portion of the study of phenomenology *has to do with examining the intention to act with an awareness of the other person (object) and the social and cultural milieu in which we do so.* It is this outward-directed notion that is most vital in my work. Actors have been harmed by the idea that somehow they must go inside themselves to find emotions. As we have been discussing, modern science indicates that almost everything we feel or experience begins outside of our body/mind. The experience of solitary confinement, the ultimate "going in" by prisoners of war suggests that without "agency" or the ability to act and without human contact, humans go mad. Prisoners left alone lose their sense of identity.[14] We also know that infants who are not picked up and held fail to develop a full sense of self, and many die even though food is available.[15] These ideas suggest that we are who we are because of our relationships and our ability to affect one another.

Emotion does not lead. The intention to act rises to the surface only after we have feelings that follow the initial sensory signals sent to the body, kicking off emotion and simultaneously preparing the body for action. In talking to young actors about this, I use a shorthand phrase (see Figure 8.2):

Image > Emo > Action

I use the word "image" broadly to mean any sensation – visual, kinesthetic, scent, auditory or other response, etc. The use of the term

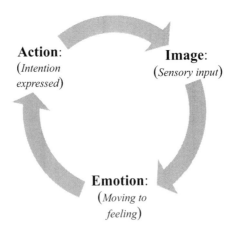

Figure 8.2 Action cycle

Created by author.

"emo" in place of "emotion" is a flag for the younger generation and helps them understand more readily. The illustration helps them to see the never-ending round dance of our lives.

The original discovery of mirror neurons (MNs) concerned a monkey (1) witnessing a scientist grasping something (I would call this an *image*), (2) feeling an emotion of desire for that object (emo), and having its brain fire in a brain location that (3) would excite action.

As this response was studied and found to exist in humans, it was quickly obvious that our actions and reactions are *inter-personally received and generated*. The monkey was responding to another being, not to a screen or to a machine. If the researcher, Vittorio Gallese, had not been moving in the room, the monkey would not have experienced the virtual action of grabbing whatever food Gallese had in his hand. For me the idea of the electronic and chemical responses to others' actions is an exciting way of looking at our interconnectedness and how we can affect audiences.

As I have been discussing, the classical idea of cognitive science sees the individual as a self-contained unit despite the research revealing that a sense of self is created through contact with others and that people isolated from human contact generally lose their sense of identity, depending on the length of time. Mirror neurons and the attendant studies have changed the entire face of the cognitive scientific community.

In an article titled *The Foundational Level of Meaning, Implicit Processes in Relation to Conflict, Defense and the Dynamic Unconscious* published in 2007 (also quoted by George Hogenson), the authors proclaim:

> Relational transaction involving action and interaction have been considered the "surface" level of meaning in previous analytic theorizing. However, the level of implicit representation encodes the most profound aspects of human experience, including the elements of conflict, defense, and affective resistance, and this level can no longer be considered "surface" or superficial. *What has arisen from the previous upside-down view of the mind is a privileging of abstraction over interaction and a privileging of the symbolic/semantic over the affective/interactive. The effect on the way psychoanalysis has been conceptualized and practiced cannot be overstated.*[16]

(author's italics)

I emphasize this point to give credence to the theory that action both implicit and explicit within a relationship is the point of acting; not psychology, not character refinement or limitation, but interaction is the point of the drama. I strongly suggest that the reader acquaint him- or herself with the article in question, which is freely available on the wonderful Research Gate website, www.researchgate.com.

Second-person interactivity: MNs

Gallese, now a world-renowned neuroscientist, recently presented a paper outlining his study of intersubjectivity from a neurological perspective. It was as revolutionary as the prior article from the *Psychoanalysis Journal*: "I challenge the standard solipsistic[17] theoretical account of intersubjectivity offered by classic cognitive science, capitalizing upon a new take on intersubjectivity, as defined by the second-person perspective."[18]

As I mentioned in the introduction to this book, my original impetus to investigate "mirror neurons" was sparked by reading Stanislavski's reference to "rays or signals."[19] The next day, I happened upon an article concerning mirror neurons (MNs). At the time, this research was just hitting the U.S. and causing quite a stir. To my way of thinking, these "rays/signals, radiating out and radiating in" were described by the mirror neurons encountered by scientists in a laboratory in Parma, Italy.

In 1996 a team of neurophysiologists led by Giacomo Rizolatti was studying the brain responses of macaque monkeys when grasping objects with their hands.

> The neurophysiologist, Vittorio Gallese was moving around the lab during a lull in the day's experiment. A monkey was sitting quietly in the chair, waiting for her next assignment. Suddenly, just as Vittorio reached for something, he does not remember what, he heard a burst of activity from the computer that was connected to the electrodes that had been surgically implanted in the monkey's brain. . . . Vittorio immediately thought the reaction was strange. The monkey was just sitting quietly, not intending to grasp anything, yet this neuron affiliated with the grasping action had fired nevertheless.[20]

What this meant was undeniable; the idea that monkey see, monkey "virtually" do is true. I believe that we now can partially understand what Stanislavski knew all along: The waves or rays are known as mirror

neurons. They are not some occult mind reading but biologically iden-
tifiable mechanisms in the brain of primates. Once again, MNs, simply
put, are elements in the brain that fire unconsciously in the presence of
another person's activity. In other words, the image of the activity creates
desire or emotion in the monkey which is translated into virtual action.

Consider a baseball fan watching a player hit a ball; fMRI (functional
magnetic resonance imaging) research shows that MNs "light" or "fire
up" in the same area of the fan's brain as those in the brain of the hitter.
The viewers of the game and the player have the same neuronal pattern
in the geography of the brain, and these are virtually synchronized by
the firing of MNs. The fans and the players are connected in this way.

Furthermore, research shows that if our fan in the stands has at
some point in life actually played baseball, the neurons will be even
more excited than those of someone who has never played or seen a
ballgame. What this implies is that we as humans respond *biologically* to recognizable actions in recognizable situations.

In order for a dramatic story to be recognizable to an audience,
actors must do actions with intentions that are meant to overcome
obstacles, just as the baseball player needs to overcome the pitcher
and the fielders by hitting, bunting, or sacrificing in order to win the
game. *Actions for actors therefore should be understood as something done either physically or verbally with the intention of effecting
change in another person.* Other "actions," such as slamming a door,
must be seen as either activities meant to communicate to someone or
something, or as famed director and acting theorist Declan Donnellan
proposes, the door might need to be given a sort of "personhood."

The use of metaphor, image, and active words

Donnellan, when commenting on *Romeo and Juliet*, discusses
Juliet's balcony as she awaits Romeo.

> Not only has the night changed but also the balcony has trans-
> formed into another stranger. Suddenly the balcony is more
> protecting, more frustrating, more silly, more important, and
> now the balcony demands to be touched or rejected, leaned on,
> stretched over, sat on or hidden behind.[21]

In seeing the balcony as an active being, Juliet's responses to it
becomes more flexible and the actress standing on it becomes far
more engaged. Juliet has not changed, the balcony has, and Juliet
must adjust to that change.

Physical reinforcement of action

As we know, scenes and acts are compilations, either linear or episodic, of actions/intentions leading to desired ends; in like manner, the aforementioned pitcher needs to strike out each batter as he comes to the plate. It therefore follows that the viewer's mirror neurons will be *physically* reinforced by the clarity of the actor's actions and intentions. This can be strengthened through the actor's commitment to finding the physical action beneath the psychology. Stanislavski said, "For my own part I would say the nearer action is to being physical the less risk you have of forcing feelings."[22]

I *contend* that language is a *calorie-saving device* whereby we *avoid* having to physically *grab, push, pull,* or otherwise get what we need from the world. Words do that for us. If an action/intention is *conceived* of corporeally (in the body), its effectiveness for the actor and for his/her partner will be *stronger* owing to the *engagement* of his MNs, which are *excited* by the images *contained in* the language itself. This idea has to do with the concept of metaphor as *employed* by Lakoff and Johnson in the book titled *Metaphors We Live By*,[23] wherein the authors *reveal* that not only do we think in metaphors far more than we may notice, but most metaphors *discard* literal thought for colorful or understandable *ways of seeing* the world.

Now look back at the prior paragraph and note the use of the words *contend, avoid, stronger, contained, employed, reveal,* and *discard.* They are words capable of being done physically. Others such as *calorie-saving, ways of seeing, engagement, conceived, excited,* and *contained in* describe things that can be viewed from a sensory or positional standpoint, i.e., up/down/over/under way. They are not literal. Examples from *Metaphors to Live By* include:

He is the *father* of modern biology.
That idea *died* on the vine.
We need to *smooth out* our differences.
Our nation *was born* out of a desire for freedom.
That's still *up in the air.*
She was *feeling down.*

Our brains are activated not only by action but also by the description of action. This concept is called embodied semantics.[24] In a study done in 2006, it was demonstrated that action words activate the part of the brain responsible for a particular part of the motor neuronal network for action. The phrase "eat a banana" activated the mouth, the phrase "push on the brake" activated the area of the brain responsible for foot movement, and so on.

Acting teachers are fond of using the concept of verbs to assist their students toward clearer work – rightly so. However, it is the quality of the vocabulary that can make the difference between a lackluster performance and one that is grounded in the actor's entire being. I have seen published lists of verbs that include, among other poorly thought out suggestions, "to inform," "to tell," and my pet bugaboo, "to explain." None of the aforementioned phrases are likely to ring any bells in the actor's body and imaginary life, and therefore no bells in the audience, either. It is physical imagery on the part of the actor that most activates his or her emotional/physical life, simply through the kinesthetic visualization necessary to conceive it. This activation is transferred via action to the audience in part using mirror neurons.

Summation

For actors, what they say is what they play. If their way of speaking to themselves contains predominantly physically conceived action/intention/image, there will be a direct and nonintellectual translation of deeply seated feelings, needs, and desires that cannot be fully verbalized. Stanislavski said, "The action precedes the feeling," which has as its correlate, "Do the action, and the emotion will emerge." These actions are revealed and understood by the audience and acting partners as a result of the activity of mirror neurons, not because of emotional content. Joseph Campbell says, in *Transformations of Myth Through Time*, "Art is the clothing of a revelation." We as theatre artists must translate into visible reality the myths and revelations presented to us by our playwrights and poets. Certainly the metaphors that surround us are a part of this revelation. When these words and images are a part of the actor's methodology, the human stories will ignite the actors and viewers far more intensely than explanation and imitation.

Memory: Images and the brain

> *We are who we are because of what we learn and what we remember.*
>
> Eric Kandel[25]

Memory was once thought to be a sort of storehouse or filing cabinet wherein full sequences or stories were filed for further use. We had very little science on the matter. For ages, repetition and rote recitation were used to implant memories of factual as well as literary ideas. Memorizing poetry as well as mathematical tables was done in the same way. Many of us in the older generation know a goodly amount of poetry as a result of this type of schooling. However, this approach is no longer taught in schools, and memorizing is seen to be detrimental to real learning because it is thought that the lack of in-depth understanding leads to fast forgetting. This is possibly true; however, I suspect because poetry, songs, and pieces of plays contain more inherent imagery, they may stick longer than other items such as dates or treaty names.

Our identity is based on our memory. Our approach to the world, our feelings about ourselves in the world, our very "me-ness" is dependent on memory. If one loses one's memory, one's sense of self goes with it. This depends on the extent of memory loss, but once we forget where we live, once we no longer recognize those dearest to us, once our short-term memory deserts us and our long-term memory begins to depart as well, we continue to function, but only as sentient beings. This is the final end of Alzheimer's disease. There is only a body left; no one is at home anymore. Consider for yourself how vital the autobiographical facts of your life are to your functioning, whether those facts are healthy or not – you are your past.

For actors, memory is not only concerned with memorizing lines and blocking, it is also necessary to create "false memories" concerning the given circumstances of the play. If an actor is to behave as if she were a courtier, she had best have images stored to allow her to behave truthfully. If not, the difficulty of learning every move and expression will overwhelm her, she will become self-conscious, and the problem will spiral down to a bad performance. If, on the other hand, the actors and the production team have taken the time to excite their body/brains with the sensory aspects of the history and art of the period, they will be able to behave in a logical manner. Some directors may say, "We don't have time for that." However, in the long run the time is actually shortened by such work, especially when done as a group and through physical activity. As the phenomenologists would say, the actors are living in the everyday world of the play with self-awareness, social awareness, spatial awareness, etc.

The push to discover the bases of memory foundation began in the early 1950s as a result of the interest in Freudian psychology as well as the Jungian school of thought. Prior to that time, there had been much thought given to how we remember, but it remained a mystery until the years between 1864 and 1879, when two areas of the cortex, Wernicke's area and Broca's area, were found to have discrete functions having to do with language comprehension and expression, respectively. Prior to that time, brain function had not been viewed as having specific locales or purposes.

However, owing to the lack of funding, world wars, and general suspicion of scientists working in the brain, the subject was left substantially unexplored. It wasn't until 1954 that neuroscientists William Scoville and Brenda Milner were able to observe an epileptic man who, after surgery to reduce his incapacitating seizures, lost his ability to remember any new information for more than a few seconds. His short-term memory had been wiped out, but his long-term memory was intact. He could remember what had happened up until the surgery, but after that he was virtually in a mixed-up sort of *Groundhog Day*.

Once this phenomenon was encountered, research began in earnest. At the same time, interest in science began to be stressed in schools, and investment in research followed. The neuronal basis of memory is now the where the action is. Researchers have divided types of memory into various categories. For the purposes of this book, it is implicit and explicit memory that we are interested in. Explicit memory is conscious and generally deals with facts, figures, and events; implicit concerns the knowledge of skills or the "how."

Many of us have heard of the method of memorizing called mnemonics (from the Greek goddess of memory, Mnemosyne, pronounced Ne-mah-zen-ee). Relating pieces of information such as a person's last name by attributing a physical characteristic or other linking device to that person is how it is done. So, as my maiden name is Drake, one might decide that I looked like a duck, and a male duck is called a drake, so the link is made. (Of course, it probably helps if you are talking also to Mr. Wolfe, and Ms. Bear, but for Ms. Syzmanski, it may be more difficult). Explicit memory is best used for facts but is not as helpful for actors wishing to memorize lines. It does, however, point us to the importance of images as essential elements of recall.

Student actors typically memorize lines by sitting at a table, generally alone, with an index card blocking the lines, trying to say them and then looking back at the page to see how well they have done. After this is accomplished, they frequently enlist the help of a roommate or spouse to sit with the pages and follow along to see if they are accurate. This teamwork may actually help a bit more because the emotionality that goes along with the interaction may assist in recall. However, the problem with all of this is that knowing the words becomes an end in itself, and the young actor winds up seeing the images of the words on the page in his/her mind rather than getting them from a need to respond to a circumstance or other stimuli. This technique forces the actor to remove him or herself metaphorically from the scene as his mind moves to find the words on the paper. "Don't tell me, I know this line. I can see it at the top of the page!"

While this does eventually fade, it takes an inordinate amount of time to do so, and the actor can end up acting alone, just her and her pages and the partner and his pages, each believing that they are communicating when nothing is being accomplished. The figurative page-wall stands between them. Many actors say, "Well, when I get 'off book,' I am much better." Certainly that is true, but this is a result of pressure to memorize rather than an understanding of how to do so.

Recently it has become fashionable for directors to ask actors to be "off book" from the first rehearsal. The scientific research on memory indicates that this is counterproductive. My own experience confirms the science of the matter. The actor spends as much time relearning what he or she believed the meaning of the line to be (and, for less well-trained actors, how it should be said) as they would if they came to rehearsal with virgin memories. This "off book" method employs explicit memory and flies in the face of cognitive science. It is can also be frustrating for those same directors, who must then break through established speech patterns to get actors to appear to be talking to each other at all.[26]

Most actors will tell you that once they have their "blocking" they can put the book down. This stands to reason; they have managed to connect meaning to movement in their bodies. This is where implicit memory takes over. Learning lines implicitly involves connecting images and motor activity to the syntax in a more natural way.

> Implicit memory is not a single memory system but a collection of processes involving several different brain systems that lie deep within the cerebral cortex. For example, the association of feelings (such as fear or happiness) with events involves a structure called the amygdala. . . . Implicit memory often has an automatic quality.

It is recalled directly through performance without any conscious effort or even awareness that we are drawing on memory.[27]

Current research has shown that memory is processed through the hippocampus, which shuttles certain experiences into the sensory areas of the amygdala, such as color, texture, light, weight, and so forth. Some are only conserved for a short term and then forgotten. The reason that one memory is stored and another rejected has to do with its connection to heightened emotion. Things that give us joy, fear, rage, grief, are signaled by stronger chemical responses having rather than have to do with pain and pleasure, survival and death. It is also the case that "where" something happens elicits synaptic connections to language and memory as well. For true memory to be implanted, the images the actor chooses must be potent and capable of exciting emotion. I use the idea of pornography. One look at a pornographic picture can change one's physiology very, very quickly.

Given the needs of the long-term memory mechanism, it seems that evoking as much physical action as possible while learning lines will entail sensory input that will in turn provoke emotion/action and ensure that the language spoken at the time of the physical action will be more clearly retained than sitting at the coffee table. This is called emotional learning.

Place and memory

Additionally, we are aware that our brains work by mapping our environments. Studies concerning "place cells" located in the hippocampus show that we map our world and the map becomes connected to our recall. This is easily recognizable if you think about driving to work or taking the bus. As you pass a certain stoplight or see a restaurant from the bus window, you may recall what you were thinking or doing in the car or on the bus at that place in the past. An actor in tech rehearsals or on a new set may be having difficulty remembering lines; it is because a change in circumstance of place or event needs to be rewired in the synapses of the memory bank.

The hippocampus does more than find places; it also stores and creates memories. Matt Wilson, a neuroscientist at the Massachusetts Institute of Technology, has found that navigation and memory are woven together in rats' brains. Place cells not only tell the rat when it's home, but also contribute to the neuronal networks responsible for encoding the memories of what happens there. So when a scent, sound, or scene triggers a recollection of home, place cells also fire.

This means that a sense of place may be evoked by an activity as much as by a physical location, and that what you do in a place affects the way you think about it. "If an animal does something different in the same place, different place cells fire," Wilson explains. "Essentially, you can change their maps and their sense of place, by simply changing what they do in that space." It's likely that the human mind operates the same way, he adds – meaning that home truly might be wherever you lay your hat. To take an everyday example, your kitchen is your kitchen because you cook in it, not just because it contains a fridge or a sink. Cooking in the kitchen helps distinguish it from your living room, Wilson says. "The fact that you do different things in them is what establishes this sense of place," he says. "Cooking is what makes your kitchen the place that it is."[28]

In other words, we identify everything through action, not language. There is another fascinating study done by scientists at Notre Dame University in 2010, with humans rather than rats, that indicates that changing the configuration of rooms or altering the layout of a room will cause us to forget things that we knew prior to the alteration. The study, titled *Walking Through Doorways Causes Forgetting*, reveals that this forgetfulness applies to objects in the room as well as language retrieval.[29]

Memory, archetype, and mirror neurons

Once again, the question of archetype needs to be revisited in relationship to both memory and archetype. According to Jungian scholar and analyst George Hogenson, archetypes are elementary action patterns such as feeding a child that are recognizable by every human even where the human has no prior experience of the act. These actions awaken instinctive archetypal visuals such as the "Eternal Mother" and either pull one toward them or push one away. They are present in the unconscious from birth as a means of structuring human behaviors when observed. They remind me of the feeling of déjà vu, in that there is an emotionally visceral response of recognition without an actual temporal experience of the oddly recalled event. They function as quasi-instincts in that they are both automatic and flexible in their cultural trappings. Using the Eternal Mother as an example, a Mother and Child in a Renaissance Painting are quite different from the same Eternal Mother concept in an ancient sculpture.

Figure 8.3 Paolo di Giovanni Fei, *Madonna and Child,* 1370s, tempera on wood, gold ground

Bequest of George Blumenthal, 1941. Courtesy of the Metropolitan Museum of Art, New York.

Figure 8.4 Yashoda with the infant Krishna, early c. twelfth century India, copper alloy

Purchase, Lita Annenberg Hazen Charitable Trust Gift, in honor of Cynthia Hazen and Leon B. Polsky, 1982. Courtesy of the Metropolitan Museum of Art, New York.

The images, while culturally and historically unrelated, are recognizable throughout the world, and the actions of feeding, cuddling, and protecting are obvious, as is the relationship therein. I would go so far as to say that it is the action in the relationship that defines the archetype.

What we have in the theory of archetypes, therefore, is a combination of features that include ways of knowing the world (patterns of apprehension and intuition – a specific subset, it seems, of ways of acting in the world), patterns of behavior, affective states that accompany these intutions and patterns of

Figure 8.5 Isis with Horus

Online Free Images from the Metropolitan Museum of Art, New York.

behavior, and finally, a notion of the image that appears to go beyond our common sense notion of the image as simply a picture or representation of some other state of affairs.[30]

In other words, archetypes function in the following ways:

- They give one a way of seeing the world without knowing the world (apprehension and intuition).
- They give one a way of acting in the world (subset).
- They elicit emotional responses (affective states).
- They are always metaphoric (beyond common sense).

Archetypes exist as a means of being safe in a world where human infants develop very slowly. They aid in predicting behavior through recognition and prior understanding of the pattern of action or behavior in question. It is not a big leap to understand that mirror neurons are a part of this process. In the paper *Archetypes as Action Patterns*, George Hogenson quotes Rizzolatti (2008, 131) in the following:

The mirror neuron system and the selectivity of the responses of the neurons that compose it, produce a shared space of action, within which each act and chain of acts, whether ours or "theirs" are immediately registered and understood without the need of any explicit or deliberate "cognitive operation."

Given the understanding that both mirror neurons and archetypal images and responses are unconscious, it then follows that for an audience to be deeply affected, the intentions revealed as a result of physically conceived action (whether externalized as gesture, completely realized, or converted to verbal energy) must be clear. Further, for the experience to be meaningfully understood, these communications must be powerfully employed.

Memory consolidation

Another part of the research into memory has to do with the length of time it takes to consolidate a memory and how best to do so. It has always been my belief that if I were hypnotized once I had attentively read something and slept on it, I would be able to recall it fully. I have never tested this theory. However, the idea is fundamentally correct. Sleeping after learning is necessary to retention. There are many studies that suggest that a power-nap after an episode of learning increases retention exponentially. And, of course, the old adage "Sleep on it" is true. It appears that REM sleep helps to strengthen memories and allows them to be retained according to their importance.

In preparing to do a scene or a play, we have discussed the efficacy of using an archetype to stimulate action. We are aware that an archetype can awaken inherently deep connections emotionally. We also know that emotion is a major component of memory composition. In a Superscene, the archetype is a spur to gross physical action and movement. Doing such strenuous activity while hearing words or phrases and repeating them will implant the language in the mind/body. When two people do a Superscene, they are learning in their bodies under a certain amount of stress. Stress of this sort and physical touch greatly improves potential for long-term memory. Long-term memory is encoded differently than short-term in the brain because it receives an extra wash of chemicals evoked by stressful emotion of the event. Emotional learning depends on high frequency stimulation of the synapses within the hippocampus to signal importance.

If, after a session of such movement/language wedding, the learner is allowed to sleep, the recall will be doubly enforced. It has been my experience that actors who engage in Superscenes have no real difficulty getting off book because they are never actually "on book." There is of course the same sort of "cleaning" that needs to be done during rehearsals for word-perfect performance, but most actors have little fear of "forgetting" because the movement of the Superscene itself has been folded into the staging.

Kindergartners take naps on rugs or blankets every day. We know they need it. Is it possible that we might forget our drive to fill every moment of rehearsal or class time with activity and let people nap for twenty minutes? Or if that is too radical, perhaps we could call it meditation and, following a scene, allow the participants to simply sit and meditate. Why is it that we, as teachers, actors, and directors, find this idea silly? We know what the science is, but we somehow believe that sleep of this kind is beneath our dignity. My students all have yoga mats; don't yours?

Notes

1 Damasio, Antonio. *Looking for Spinosa: Joy, Sorrow, and the Feeling Brain*. First Harvest ed. Orlando: Harcourt Books, 2003.
2 LeDoux, Joseph. *The Emotional Brain: The Mysterious Underpinnings of Emotional Life*. New York: Simon and Schuster Paperbacks, 1996.
3 In response to the writings of Charles Darwin, John Dewey outlined these ideas in *Psychology Review* in three articles: The Theory of Emotion: (1) Emotional Attitudes, vol 1 / issue #1, 1894, 553–559; The Theory of Emotion: (2) The Significance of Emotion, vol 2 / issue #1, January 1895, 13–32; and The Reflex Arc Concept in Psychology, vol 3 / issue #4, July 1896, 357–370.
4 Alcoholics Anonymous. *The Big Book*. 4th ed. New York: Alcoholics Anonymous Publishing, 2001.
5 Donnellan, Declan. *The Actor and the Target*. Great Britain: Nick Hern and Theatre Communications Group, 2002, 33.
6 Carnicke, Sharon. *Stanislavski in Focus*. London: Routledge Press, 2003.
7 Brewer, Judson A., P.D. Worhunsky, J.R. Gray, Y.Y. Tang, J. Weber, and H. Kober. (2011). Meditation Experience Is Associated with Differences in Default Mode Network Activity and Connectivity. *Proceedings of the National Academy of Sciences of the United States of America* 108 (50), 20254–20259.

8 Ibid.
9 Dennett, Daniel C. (1993). Review of Varela: The Embodied Mind. *American Journal of Psychology* 106, 121–126.
10 Smith, David Woodruff. *Phenomenology: The Stanford Encyclopedia of Philosophy*, December 16, 2013. http://plato.stanford.edu/entries/phenomenology.
11 Ibid.
12 Varela, Francisco, Evan Thompson, and Eleanor Rosch. *The Embodied Mind: Cognitive Science and Human Experience*. Rev ed. Cambridge, MA: MIT Press, 1992.
13 Dennett, Review of Varela.
14 Spitz, R.A. (1945). Hospitalism: An Inquiry Into the Genesis of Psychiatric Conditions in Early Childhood. *Psychoanalytic Study of the Child* 1, 53–74.
15 Ibid.
16 Stern, D.D.N., Sander, L.W., Nahum, J.P., Harrison, A.M., Lyons-Ruth, K., Morgan, A.C. et al. (2007). The Foundational Level of Psychodynamic Meaning: Implicit Processes in Relation to Conflict Defense and the Dynamic Unconscious. *International Journal of Psychoanalysis* 88, I–16.
17 Merriam Webster. Solipsism: A theory in philosophy that your own existence is the only thing that is real or that can be known.
18 Phil. Trans. R. Soc. B 2014 369, 20130177, published 28 April 2014.
19 Stanislavski, Konstantin. *An Actor's Work*, trans. Jean Benedetti. New York: Routledge Press, 2008.
20 Iacoboni, Mario. *Mirroring People*. New York: Farrar, Straus and Giroux, 2008.
21 Donnellan, Declan. *The Actor and the Target*. London: Nick Hern Books, 2005, 136.
22 Stanislavski, *An Actor's Work*.
23 Lakoff, George and Johnson, Mark. *Metaphors We Live By*. Chicago: University of Chicago Press, 1980.
24 Current Biology 16. *Congruent Embodied Representations for Visually Presented Actions and Linguistic Phrases Describing Actions. 1818–1823.* Elsevier. September 19, 2006. http://www.sciencedirect.com/science/article/pii/S0960982206019683.
25 Kandel, Eric. *In Search of Memory: The Emergence of a New Science of the Mind*. New York: W.W. Norton & Co., 2006.
26 There is also an ethical question when it comes to requiring professional actors to work without being paid, which is basically what occurs in this instance. Additionally, many theatres and directors expect actors to be "off book" for auditions. This practice is a problem for more reasons than I have time to elucidate.
27 Kandel, *In Search of Memory*, 132.
28 Costandi, Moheb. Emotional Renovations: How Your Brain Twists Together Emotion and Place. *Nautilus Quarterly*, 2013. http://nautil.us/issue/8/home/emotional-renovations.
29 Radvansky, G., Krawietz, S., and Tamplin, A. (2011). Walking Through Doorways Causes Forgetting: Further Explorations. *The Quarterly Journal of Experimental Psychology* 64 (8), 1632–1645.
30 Hogenson, George. (2009). Archetypes as Action Patterns. *Journal of Analytical Psychology* 1 (54), 325–337.

Appendix

Stanislavski Chart

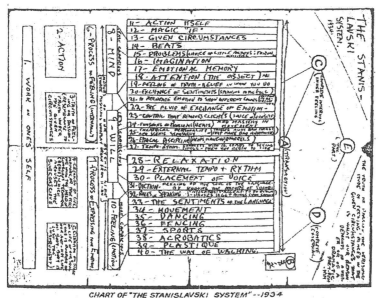

CHART OF "THE STANISLAVSKI SYSTEM"--1934

Jeff Zinn, director and acting pedagogue, included this chart in his wonderful book, *The Existential Actor* (Smith and Kraus, 2015, p. 70). He goes on to say:

> It would fall to Stanislavski's descendants – Lee Strasberg, Stella Adler, Sanford Meisner, Uta Hagen – to transform the *system* into a *method*. Each of them would draw from the system the element they felt was most central and essential, in many cases leaving the rest behind.

The chart is a comprehensive overview of the various elements essential to the practice of acting. That being said, I agree with Zinn that it is "almost overwhelming in its breadth and complexity." It is not intended to be used by actors per se; rather it is a sort of "good acting" check list and a cheat sheet when things are going wrong. As an acting teacher and director, I have used it in such a way, but I do not usually give it to actors to study. Its overly intellectual look at the art and craft is dangerous in the wrong hands! The chart is meant to be read from the bottom up, starting with #1 "Work on One's Self." "Action" is number two. This places use of one's self and action in a dominant position. At the very top of the chart, beyond the thirteen elements in their columns, is the word "transaction." Transaction in this setting means the transactions between and among the elements but also implies "interaction" between and among the characters in a play. The columns describe the elements needed to perfect the actions and transactions to end up with "The Part."

I had never seen this chart until I was older, and it remains meaningful to me, but had I encountered it earlier, it might have been too much of a muchness to tolerate.

Chapter 9

Archetypal patterns

Archetypes are a space for the imagination. They open out to the world. The use of archetypes by theatre practitioners can lift the work out of psychology and debate and thrust it into active images and understandings. Because archetypes are universal and easily understood, they enable actors of any level to quickly find their way through scripts that may seem impenetrable. While many theorists have attempted to list or describe these structures or forms, it must be understood that there can be no finite list of ways of responding to the world. In this chapter, I am including some lists, but they are alterable and finite, unlike the gods and heroes they represent.

Family stories

In order for any archetypes to be revealed in either Jungian shadow or self, they must be seen in conflict with the world, specifically with other people. All stories are constructed based in familial understandings, and each relationship has its concomitant conflict that highlights the actions contained in the archetypes. The archetypal relationships that form the mythic primordial soup of any story are all first encountered in the family. Here is a list of these, along with the general conflict. A word of warning: The fact of a relationship is not always the truth of the relationship, and that is often a subject of drama. For instance, when King Lear becomes childish, he is no longer a parent, and all hell breaks loose as a result.

1 Parents and children: Independence versus freedom
2 Siblings: Status
3 Extended family: Help versus hindrance
4 Husbands and wives: Power balance

5   Friends of the same sex: Competition versus support
6   Friends of the opposite sex: Sex versus friendship
7   Lovers: Commitment
8   And, possibly, God: Love versus vengeance

We are born helpless, dependent on our Mother or principal care-giver in order to maintain our existence. Our first relationship is with her and our first conflict is with her. A hungry infant needs milk when it is hungry, and this hunger may not coincide with the Mother's ability to attend to the child – or an infant may want cuddling or rocking when another child is being held; both instances cause frustration, pain, and conflict. Our Father, if he is present, takes Mother from us, even though he can often be useful for entertainment, comfort, or instruction, but if we want Mother, we don't want Father. Siblings too may be entertaining or instructive, helpful, and nurturing and may also stand between us and Mother or Father. As we mature, we enlarge the circle of people in our families from whom we can receive nurturing, both emotional and physical. We learn what Mom likes and how to behave to get our treats. We learn how to avoid the anger of our siblings or how to best them; we learn how to wrap Dad around our little fingers. We find that a Grandfather can substitute for a missing Father; we learn that we are pleasing to the eye or that we are smart or charming or powerful. By the age of 5, we have determined how to relate to the world of men and women through our childhood community of parents, siblings, and extended family. Our patterns of responding to the world are in our consciousness before we have achieved full consciousness, and how we get what we want is a result primarily of these childhood experiences.

Each relationship contains within it the seeds of its own destruction. We see such conflicts every day in the advice columns: sibling rivalries based on the "Mom or Dad always loved you best" theory, dominating parental figures still controlling their adult children's lives, parents who never loved enough, children who rebel and strike out, dependent siblings who lean on each other until one breaks, silent husbands and noisy wives, lovers who are only able to give a teaspoon full of love but who need a gallon for themselves, spouses, partners who stray. The audience's point of contact with the play and its people is the recognition of these archetypal relationships and their concomitant conflicts.

All of these relational problems are preexisting conditions; like a heart condition that is revealed only under stress, the conflicts inherent in the relationships may lie undiagnosed until something happens. That *something* is the plot that serves to reveal the conflict by turning up the heat from simmer to boil. While Aristotle may say that plot is more important than character, I think he failed to consider that there is a plot already in place, a plot that speaks to us on an archetypal level: The plot of the relationship.

Summation

Relationships are by their very nature conflicted and, it is the particularity of this conflict that reveals the relationship. Cain will always fight with Abel – it is the ancient story of brother against brother – and parents will always come to conflict with children attempting to establish independent identities – it is a hallmark of the relationship. The actor must concern himself with seeking the conflict in the relationship that exists *external* to the situation in the play in order to create deeply recognizable life on stage – relationships which exist before the plot and continue to exist after it. The plot only serves to ignite the conflict which lies hidden under social faces.

C.G. Jung

The psychoanalyst and colleague of Freud's who first brought the word archetype to prominence believed that there were twelve basic archetypes recognizable to all of us. He was not the first to use the word, but he was the first to bring the ideas into the body as essential ways of thinking and seeing. For him, these roles contain the basic structures of all relationships and behavior. His overarching idea was that humans were divided in a sense into the anima, or feminine, and the animus, or masculine. These simplifications must not be misunderstood. While it is undoubtedly true that Jung was working within a male culture and focused on what he considered masculine behavior, he did not see women or the female as inferior. However, it is true that he was far more concerned with defining his terms from a masculine perspective.

The anima and the animus are not directives for how to behave, nor are they gendered except in the language employed. Simply put, they are the repressed "feminine" residing in every male and the repressed "masculine" residing in every female below the level of consciousness. They concern the way in which a woman may perceive maleness as *other* than herself and the way a man may view femaleness as *other* than himself. The anima or the animus may be seen as the "shadow" of the presented self, and it is only through merging with the shadow, or joining anima to animus, that Jung believed full selfhood was achieved.

For Jung, the anima is expressed by males in four archetypes. The modern references are mine.

- Eve: Great Mother of Nature – Sophia Lauren, Dolly Parton, Queen Elizabeth I.
- Sophia: Spiritual Woman of Wisdom, Crone – Mother Teresa, Eleanor Roosevelt, Aung Sang Suu Kyi, Maya Angelou.
- Helen: Beauty, Energy Without the Requirement of Virtue. As Harold Bloom says, "Beauty writes its own laws." – Marilyn Monroe, Princess Diana, Grace Kelly.
- Mary: Woman of Virtue, a subset of Eve, but without sin – Helen Keller, Joan of Arc.

Jung didn't define the animus nearly as clearly from a female perspective, perhaps because he was living in a male body in a male culture. However, he did create the following identifications.

- Man of mere physical power: Tarzan, Arnold Schwarzenegger, Hercules, Wesley Snipes, Jackie Chan, The Rock.
- Man of action or romance: Robin Hood, Superman, Prince Hal, Indiana Jones, James Dean, Agent 007, Cary Grant, Brad Pitt.
- Man as professor, clergyman, orator: President Obama, Atticus Finch, Martin Luther King Jr., Wole Soyinka.
- Man as guide and holder of wisdom: Billy Graham, Buddha, Carl Sagan, Morgan Freeman, Gandhi, Nelson Mandela.

These categories each have a "shadow" or opposite within itself, thus becoming archetypes rather than stereotypes.

- Eve opposite – Lilith: Knowing Sexuality and Equality with Adam, Cause of all Sin – Madonna, Pam Grier, Jane Russell, Lady Gaga, Josephine Baker.
- Sophia opposite – Witch, Hag: Black Magic through Occult Knowledge – Imelda Marcos, Leona Helmsley, Mrs. Mao Zedong.
- The Great Mother opposite – The Devouring Mother: Capable of eating her young – Amy Chua (Tiger Mother), Regina Giddens (Little Foxes), Joan Crawford, Winnie Mandela. This is probably the most frightening of all archetypes.

For the male archetypes:

- Man of mere physical power opposite: Weak or Fearful Coward – This is an interesting type; very hard to find any famous chickens besides Achilles (Iliad), The cowardly lion, Lance Armstrong, any number of politicians.
- Man of action or romance opposite: Cynical Intellectual – William Buckley, Humphrey Bogart, Bill Murray.
- Man as professor, clergyman, orator opposite: Pretender to Knowledge or Spiritual Qualities – Jimmy Swaggart, Bill Cosby.
- Man as guide and holder of wisdom opposite: Seducer, Liar – Jim Jones of the Jonestown massacre, Bernie Madoff; many molesters who are teachers or priests fall under this rubric.

Inherent in all of these Jungian archetypes are the following:

The Father–Protector opposite: Persecutor.
The Child–Innocent opposite: Sophisticate.
The Maiden–Virgin opposite: Whore.
The Devil–Evil incarnate opposite: Remorseful Fallen Angel or God.
God opposite: The Devil; however, God often has no opposite except in humans' belief in the difference between an avenging God and a merciful God. Hitler might fit into this Devil category.
The Wise Old Woman or Man opposite: Sinful User of Knowledge for Selfish Ends.
The Trickster–A wise fool opposite: True Companion.
The Hero–Noble seeker of knowledge and justice opposite: Ignoble Betrayer.

Archetypal patterns of plots

While I know that there are many theorists who have taken the time to count the number of stories or conflicts, the gentlemen below are the ones with whom I am most familiar. Given the fact that there are perhaps six or seven potential human relationships, it seems obvious that these storylines must be limited to some arithmetic permutation of these. In reading these lists, it is also apparent that all of these begin with an ancient story that has been passed down from the early light of our human existence.

Georges Polti did a rather complete analysis of plots in 1921 and determined that there were thirty-six of them.[1] The titles of these are not in fact stories; they are mostly actions or in some cases emotional difficulties. Polti lists the essential characters needed to bring the stories suggested by them to life. For my money, Polti is the best of these scholars and philosophers because he understands conflict.

Polti's thirty-six dramatic situations

(Polti includes the relationship needed to create the plot.)

1 Supplication – Persecutor, Suppliant, a Power in Authority
2 Deliverance – Unfortunates, Threatener, Rescuer
3 Revenge – Avenger, Criminal
4 Vengeance by Family upon Family – Avenging Kinsman, Guilty Kinsman, Relative
5 Pursuit – Fugitive from Punishment, Pursuer
6 Victim of Cruelty or Misfortune – Unfortunates, Master or Unlucky Person
7 Disaster – Vanquished Power, Victorious Power or Messenger
8 Revolt – Tyrant, Conspirator(s)
9 Daring Enterprise – Bold Leader, Goal, Adversary
10 Abduction – Abductor, Abducted, Guardian
11 Enigma – Interrogator, Seeker, Problem
12 Obtaining – Two or more Opposing Parties, Object, maybe an Arbitrator
13 Familial Hatred – Two Family Members who hate each other
14 Familial Rivalry – Preferred Kinsman, Rejected Kinsman, Object
15 Murderous Adultery – Two Adulterers, the Betrayed
16 Madness – Madman, Victim
17 Fatal Imprudence – Imprudent person, Victim or lost object
18 Involuntary Crimes of Love – Lover, Beloved, Revealer
19 Kinsman Kills Unrecognised Kinsman – Killer, Unrecognized Victim, Revealer
20 Self-Sacrifice for an Ideal – Hero, Ideal, Person or Thing Sacrificed
21 Self-Sacrifice for Kindred – Hero, Kinsman, Person or Thing Sacrificed

22 All Sacrificed for Passion – Lover, Object of Passion, Person or Thing Sacrificed
23 Sacrifice of Loved Ones – Hero, Beloved Victim, Need for Sacrifice
24 Rivalry Between Superior and Inferior – Superior, Inferior, Object
25 Adultery – Deceived Spouse, Two Adulterers
26 Crimes of Love – Lover, Beloved, theme of Dissolution
27 Discovery of Dishonor of a Loved One – Discoverer, Guilty One
28 Obstacles to Love – Two Lovers, Obstacle
29 An Enemy Loved – Beloved Enemy, Lover, Hater
30 Ambition – An Ambitious Person, Coveted Thing, Adversary
31 Conflict with a God – Mortal, Immortal
32 Mistaken Jealousy – Jealous One, Object of Jealousy, Supposed Accomplice, Author of Mistake
33 Faulty Judgment – Mistaken One, Victim of Mistake, Author of Mistake, Guilty Person
34 Remorse – Culprit, Victim, Interrogator
35 Recovery of a Lost One – Seeker, One Found
36 Loss of Loved Ones – Kinsman Slain, Kinsman Witness, Executioner

Denis Johnson, American Playwright and Novelist, National Book Award Winner

Johnson has published a list of nine basic plots.[2] None of these are plots; they are archetypal characters who need other archetypal characters for the story to come to life. I have taken the liberty of filling in the needed casts:

1 Cinderella: Unrecognized virtue – *Needs* wicked stepsisters, stepmother, prince, and fairy godmother.
2 Achilles: Hero with a fatal flaw – *Needs* a lot of Greek warriors, Patroclus, Hector, and others to see his inability to control himself.
3 Faust: A debt that must be paid – *Needs* the Devil to pay, and lots of sexy girls.
4 Tristan and Isolde: Love triangle – This is a twofer. There is a preexisting conflict between Tristan and Isolde, and there must be the person in the ménage, namely Isolde's husband, the king.

5   Circe: Spider and the fly – *Needs* Odysseus, who enters the web, and probably his shipmates who join in.

6   Romeo and Juliet: Star-crossed lovers – *Needs* parents, the Friar, the Duke, and friends to help or hinder, in addition to their own basic conflict, i.e., order/chaos.

7   Orpheus: A gift that is taken away – *Needs* the taker! Ah yes, but why is it taken away? What was the gift? The music or Eurydice? Or was it just Venus being jealous? Or Hades cursing him? This would make a great improv.

8   Indiana Jones: Indomitable hero – *Needs* someone to dominate! Mr. Jones can only be indomitable if there is the always-faithful woman, the villainous Nazi; who?

9   The Wandering Jew: A man cursed by the gods to wander the earth – *Needs* people out to persecute and shun him, or we will not know he is cursed or wandering.

Christopher Booker[3]

[Again I have taken the liberty of commenting on this list and supplying a few examples.]

1   Man vs. Man. The problem is another character. *Example*: Bob needs to defeat Alice to become class president. *In a play, all problems stem from perceived problems with another character, even if that character is called God or the Government or Fate.*

2   Man vs. Self. The problem lies inside the protagonist. *Example*: Bob doesn't know how to express his emotions to Alice. *However, the problem within can only be recognized when it is externalized. If not, we have a novel. It is not able to be dramatized until the problem emerges in the scenes with Alice.*

3   Man vs. Nature. The problem comes from natural sources. *Example*: A volcano destroys Bob's town, or Alice is stricken with cancer. *The volcano becomes a "person" or an uncaring god psychologically in this sort of tale, as does Alice's disease.*

4   Man vs. Society. The problem is the social environment. *Example*: Alice struggles to maintain her dignity in a sexist community. *There must be a personal representative of the sexist community for this story to be put on stage. And it only takes a little time for us to discover that the sexism is perhaps a political problem of power, or inherent male difficulties.*

5 Man vs. God/Fate. The problem is destiny, eventuality, fate, or divine will. *Example:* Bob does not want to fulfill a prophecy that he will lose his family. *See #3.*

6 Man caught in the Middle (of other characters/conflicts). *Example:* Bob gets involved in Alice's fight with her mother. *The hero is always caught in the middle of other characters or conflicts. A story does not require a self-motivated hero, or one who wants to go on an adventure.*

Notes

1 Polti, Georges. *The Thirty-Six Dramatic Situations*, trans. Lucile Ray. Franklin, OH: James Knapp Reeve, 1921.

2 Johnson list found in Parker, Philip. *The Art and Science of Screenwriting.* 2nd ed. Exeter, U.K.: Intellect, 1999.

3 Booker, Christopher. *The Seven Basic Plots.* London: Bloomsbury Academic Publishing, 2006.

Chapter 10

Archetypal journey: *In the Blood* by Suzan-Lori Parks

In the Blood by Suzan-Lori Parks is a modern tragedy featuring an underclass heroine, Hester La Negrita, who is an unmarried mother with five children. I suggest that you purchase your own copy; however, it is available for free online in a heavily annotated article at http://www.ccsenet.org/journal/index.php/ells/article/viewFile/17565/11721.

If I were reading this book, I might be tempted to skip this chapter, but I hope you don't do so. The play and its ancient roots are so rich that you do yourself a disservice if you dismiss it. I will try to keep the writing lively! Suzan-Lori Parks is one of the best playwrights in America today, and knowing her work has enriched my life.

The play is based on *The Scarlet Letter*, a short novel by Nathaniel Hawthorne that fascinated Parks to such a degree that she wrote two different plays based on it, *Fucking A* and *In the Blood*. The story of Hester is certainly mythological in essence, dealing with the denial of nature, references to treasure and gold, time, sex of all kinds, exile, the hand of fate, Hercules's club, and other elements of this kind. I include it in the book because it doesn't fit the narrative pattern of the journey, even though it includes many elements. In the Hero's Journeys, male or female, things may happen repeatedly or slightly out of order. The main issue is that a Journey proceeds from Separation to Initiation to Return.

It can be looked at many ways:

- Literally, it is a warning to women to avoid premarital sex.
- Psychologically, Hester can be seen as progressively growing into a dissociated and murderous paranoiac, which may be genetic.
- Sociologically, it is a comment on maddening the problems presented to the impoverished by the poor and undereducated.

- Politically, it is an indictment of capitalism, the disempowerment of its bureaucrats and helpers, and the inevitability of poverty in such a structure.
- Mythologically, it can be seen as the working of fate on a woman cursed by whatever gods she has offended.
- Universally, it can be seen as the disaster caused when nature is thwarted by human intervention. The order needed by capitalism, by overpopulation, by overmechanization requires fences and robots; the order of nature requires freedom, blood, and passion.

The ancient story, myth, and archetype

The cursed Hester La Negrita was never a part of the society, as Hawthorne's heroine had been. She is an oddly pure and innocent being in a world of stench and defilement, and as the archetypal goddess that she is, she has power over both life and death. Her tragedy is that she is also part mortal. When she kills her son, she is as maddened as the Maenads. All the males in her world have injured her. Her son, Jabber, is growing to become a man who will condemn her with the word SLUT, and she slays him, which as she would have the other men in her life. She doesn't know that he is Jabber; he is simply a male spirit, a spirit that wishes to destroy her powers, and she can't allow it. Her grief upon discovery is profound, and the gods punish her for her crime, just like Pentheus's mother, Agave, in *The Bacchae*. Hester's tragic flaw is expectation of honor in a world that no longer finds children and childbirth sacred.

Hester is a woman doing exactly what nature and her biology have meant her to do – have sex joyfully and freely and produce healthy babies. She is essentially serving the ancient Great Goddess who celebrates fecundity. In the eyes of the original Goddess religion, the men who fathered children were simply sperm donors and were free to go, having done their duty. In fact, historically, once a donor had served his year as consort, he was often killed. That this is no longer possible does not mean that the call of Cybele, the tripartite Goddess, is not being heard.

Hester has been born out of her time, and her inability to deal with employment, the alphabet, writing, and subsidized housing emerges not from a lack on her part but from the sheer incomprehensibility of it to her life. It is as if she is a visitor in a bleak place and cannot really grasp how such a world is possible. She expects to be taken care of by her community, as she would have been in ancient times. She expects the world to see sex as a gift rather than as an exchange. She does not wish to be paid for it; she is a holy woman who gives it freely. When she begins to awaken to the reality of her situation, she attempts to trade sex and to work within the system, such as it is. The compromises are too much for her, and she loses her mind.

Protagonist/antagonist statement

These are various ways of looking at the play:

- Hester, needing to fulfill her sacred duty and give the gift of children to the world, tries to get a "leg up" from her community, but the community, wanting to destroy her ability to have more children, threatens to remove her reproductive organs, resulting in Hester's going mad and killing her first and most beloved child.
- Hester, needing Jabber to be her best support, resists Jabber's desire to make her independent and civilized, but Jabber, wanting to make his mother independent, forces her to face facts, resulting in Hester's killing Jabber.
- The sacred goddess, needing to fulfill her holy function and have as many children as possible, seeks humans to support her, but the humans who hate the goddess, having turned to a male god of material goods, decide to destroy her powers, resulting in the goddess turning into a vengeful monster and destroying the best of her children.
- Mother Nature, wanting to fulfill her need to be abundant, strives to give birth to as many things as possible because the ecology is threatened, but civilization, needing to control nature, puts boundaries and controls on nature, resulting in Nature's seeking revenge on civilization with every tool at her command.

Hester's Hero's Journey

Choral prologue

Innocent world of childhood

Hester appears with a newborn after the chorus is done. Just as in *The Scarlet Letter*, she raises her Child to the sky gods. There are many cultures that lift the child to the sky; most of these seem to be centered in Africa, and sometimes the father does this alone,

Table 10.1 Gods: *In the Blood*

Character	Archetype	Shadow	Familial
Hester	Eve, Great Mother	Monster Mother	Mother
Jabber	Child	Sophisticate, Manipulator	Son
Amiga Gringa	Lilith	Eve	Sister
Welfare	Wise Woman	Wicked Witch	Grandmother
Doctor	Guide and Holder of Wisdom	Seducer, Liar, Conspirator	Lover
Reverend	Man of Spirit, Orator	False Prophet	Father
Chilli	Man of Romance or Action	Cynical Betrayer, Exploiter	Husband

sometimes joined by the mother. It is thought that Roman fathers did the same. Hester: *My Treasure My Joy.*

Scene one: Under the bridge

There is a goodly amount of foreshadowing here and a relationship to folk tales, not only in the "fairy tale" that Hester gives to the children but also in the many references to *fairies and gold.*

As a female hero, Hester begins in an *enclosure* under a bridge, the gray world of the female Hero's Journey. This is not an unusual trope in mythology for women. She has five children all of whom have names defining their qualities in relationship to Hester and the other children. None have actual proper names.

Hester is seen at "home" with Baby, and son Jabber in *the inno-cent world of childhood.* Specifically, Jabber is asking her to work on her letters, but she prefers to play. The word SLUT remains on the wall. Jabber attempts to get Hester to write, but refuses to tell her what *the writing on the wall means.* Mythologically, the writing on the wall is always an *omen of doom.*

Her other children, named Bully, Beauty, and Trouble, enter, hav-ing run from a cop who was chasing them. Trouble has stolen a club from the policeman. Hester takes it from him and tucks it into her waist. She is *arming herself with a traditionally male weapon;* the club is a symbol of Hercules. In doing so, she is claiming her shadow, or animus, however unknowingly.

Call to adventure

Amiga Gringa brings news that Chilli is back in town.
Inciting incident. This news puts Hester into high gear.

Refusal of the call

Hester denies Amiga's news of Chilli.

Amiga: Word is that yr first love is back in town, doing well and
         looking for you. [Chilli]
Hester: Bullshit. Gimme my money.

Acceptance of the call

Amiga suggests to Hester that she should go to the Reverend because
he has money now. Amiga Gringa gives Hester a payment for a
watch that Hester has found on the street, but keeps a good amount
of it. Hester was expecting more money. *Desire for* **treasure.**

Hester does not want to leave home and so depends on Amiga for
news and to do business, which is not in the female world in any event
which is not an element of the goddess's worldview.

The gods send *another messenger*: The Doctor who announces
that her yearly check-up is due. Amiga scores some drugs from him,
revealing him to be a persecutor as well as a healer.

The children get out of bed at that moment, and the *Monster
Mother emerges*:

Hester: To Trouble: You sleepwalk yrself back over here and
            gimmie them matches or Ima kill you.
To Trouble: Go inside and lie down and shut up or you wont see
            tomorrow.
To Jabber: Yeah you should now cause yr uh damn accident!

It seems as if Hester decides to get money from the Reverend to
spiff herself up for Chilli. Hester says, "His heart is real hard, like a
rock." Amiga Gringa says, "Worth a try all the same." Hester then
says, "Who told you Chilli was looking for me?"

Scene two: Street practice

Crossing the first threshold

Hester *ventures out of her cave into the world* to see if she can get
money from the Reverend. She needs *treasure*, which equals freedom for her.

On the way, she encounters the Doctor (*a magical messenger from the gods or "higher ups" who determine one's fate*), and after a humiliating examination she learns that she is going to have a hysterectomy because she has had too many children. She is literally going to be dismembered. The Doctor behaves like a mechanic, not a medical man.

She offers herself to him, but he refuses her. He says that if she names the father of Baby, she may be able to avoid the operation.

Hester: "You said you was lonesome once. I came for a checkup and you said you was lonesome. You lonesome today, Doc."

Doc: "No."

Scene three: The Reverend on his soapbox

Tests and ordeals: Dragon battle #1 – The Reverend

Hester confronts The Reverend, *but he denies his fatherhood and rebukes her, telling her to come back later*, and he will give her more money than Welfare would.

Scene four: With the Welfare

Tests and ordeals: Dragon battle #2 – Welfare

Welfare visits Hester, where she ridicules and threatens Hester with "spaying." She takes sexual advantage, a form of *rape trauma* often found in female journeys, and tries to extort more favors, holding the "spaying" over her head. She also suggests that if Hester names Baby's father, she would get $100 more, although there would be a finder's fee. Welfare offers her a job sewing a dress (a challenge) that is clearly impossible, but Hester takes it. *This is not a labor that Hester can succeed in, but she accepts.*

Crisis: This is the beginning of her true descent into madness.

The *Monster Mother goddess* begins to emerge as Hester threatens to hurt Welfare.

Hester (to Welfare): Don't Make me hurt you.
I didn't mean it. Just slipped out.
Hester (to Welfare): Don't Make me hurt you.

The children are playing with cars, saying "Red light. Green light. Red light. Green light."

It is sometime after this and before scene five that Hester sees an eclipse. She says it happened as she was crossing the street. As we never see her do so, I am postulating that the children's game coupled with the torture by Welfare give her this image. This may be the traffic to which Hester refers in the next scene with the Reverend.

It is also possible on a literal level that she has a stroke and that the light and dark of the eclipse are neurological in nature. Both could be true. Hester, who has been bent over with pain in her stomach, spots Chilli as she recovers from her attack. She screams *"Chilli!"*

Scene five: Small change and sandwiches

Tests and ordeals: Amiga's challenges

Amiga *tests* Hester, suggesting that she can sell the fabric for her for $100, which is far more than Welfare will pay, and that she abandon the attempt to work within the system. Hester can be seen as *reverting* here as she tries to work within the system once again.

Hester shares with Amiga that she has seen Chilli and that he looks rich. She also reports that she has seen "the e-clipse," which is ignored by Amiga. An eclipse is typically a mythological warning of the end of the world.

Amiga tells Hester she is pregnant and she may sell the child (the implication is that the child is Jabber's). Amiga attempts to kiss Hester (who refuses), then she eats a part of Hester's sandwich, and ends by grabbing the fabric that Welfare has given Hester to sew and taking it with her.

MONSTER GODDESS REAPPEARS

Hester (to Amiga Gringa):   Cheat me and I'll kill ya.

Scene six: The Reverend on the rock

Tests and ordeals: Dragon battle #3 – The Reverend

RECOGNITION OF THE SEDUCER

Hester visits the Reverend, who once again denies her *and forces her to have oral sex with him*. This rape is actually accomplished rather than suggested in the text. Despite this, *she offers herself again* (more reversion), but he tells her to go home, offering her some money. He says that in the future if she wants more money, she should come around the back of his church. *She reports that she has seen an eclipse. He denies that an eclipse has occurred.*

Scene seven: My song in the street

Tests and ordeals: Chilli, demon lover

Hester and the children pay freeze tag, and Hester freezes looking up at the sun. Bully says, "She's having a nervous breakdown." The children ignore their mother's distress while they discuss sex in a very mechanistic fashion. She sees **the hand of Fate** is reaching for her.

Meeting with the Erotic and Romantic Man of Action: Hester is reunited with her lover. They experience a moment of joy, and he leaves her because of her children.

THE HAND OF FATE APPEARS AGAIN

Hester, again the *Monster Mother Goddess*, becomes more unsettled. She raises her hand to Trouble, who runs off. "Don' make me hurt you."

The children leave and Hester stands transfixed by the sun's rays and the blot she imagines is there. "Big dark thing. God's hand. Coming down on me. Blocking the light out. 5-fingered hand of fate. Coming down on me."

Demon Messenger: The Doctor enters and announces that the date of her hysterectomy has been decided. "Day after tomorrow."

Scene eight: The Reverend on the rock

Tests and ordeals: Dragon battle #4 – The Reverend

Hester returns to the Reverend for her money. He lies to her about it. She attempts to seduce him, hoping that sex will stop the hand of fate from coming down. He refuses; she moves to hit him with her club, and as he is stronger than she, he brutally twists her hand.

CATASTROPHE

The *Monster Mother has taken over*, and Hester gives in to her rage.

Reverend (to Hester): "Slut." Rest "Don't come back here again!
Ever! Y'll never get nothing from me! Common Slut. Tell on me! Go
on! Tell the world! I'll crush you underfoot." He leaves.

Symbolic death and dismemberment

CLIMAX

Hester kills Jabber in a fit of madness as he repeatedly screams "*Slut*"
at her.
    She fulfills her fate in killing her son and metaphorically herself.
    Hester has lost her fight against the world and will not be able to
fulfill her heroine's destiny. But wow, did she ever fight.

DENOUEMENT

The Doctor and Welfare discuss Hester's fate, and she can only look
at her bloody arms and say, "Big hand coming down on me."

There Was an Old Woman

This folk poem is referred to by Amiga Gringa in an early scene. It
is a piece of folk culture, with no known author.

> *There was an old woman who lived in a shoe.*
> *She had so many children, she didn't know what to do;*
> *She crummed 'em some porridge (or gave them very little*
>   *porridge)*
> *without any bread;*
> *And she borrow a beetle (a wooden club)*
> *and she knocked 'em all on the head [or]*
> *(Then whipped them all soundly)*
> *and put them to bed.*
> *Then out went th' old woman to bespeak 'em a coffin,*
> *And when she came back, she found 'em all a-loffe'n.*

(loffening = laughing, according to Mary Elizabeth Wright's *Rustic
Speech and Folklore*)

Chapter 11

Conclusion

My Hero's Journey was begun many years ago when I first witnessed a Hamlet standing under a light and wondering what he should do. I knew from that time what I wanted to do. I wanted to act, but more, I wanted to be a citizen of the theatre; I wanted to be a part of a world that could so easily transport both myself and others to imaginary places of wisdom and beauty safely.

I have arrived back home from my journey and know that I must bring back to my community of theatre artists what I learned along the way. It is my hope that those behind me on the road can take my knowledge and put it to use in whatever way they deem fit and to expand my searches for all of us.

As I said in the beginning, I am not a scientist and not a true scholar. Everything that I have done has been for the betterment of actors and directors within my limited circle. I am neither a New Yorker nor a Los Angelino; my work has been done in the midwest and in the south. I realize that this will have an effect on how well this book does in the wider world. I have never achieved fame or fortune, but I have proudly affected the lives of thousands of actors, and it is to them I must at least in part dedicate this book and my work.

Actors are the most over- and underqualified people in a theatre that seems to be based on the idea that the directors are the people with all the answers. While collaboration is generally the stated aim of an artistic group, it often becomes manipulation of the actor through exercises and rehearsals designed to realize only a director's vision that has been determined months or years earlier. By the time most actors are on board, their intellectual input is often dismissed because the director has already made up his or her mind as to what the actor must do and how. The real statement concerning collaboration is: "I want you to find a way to do it my way." However, the Merriam-Webster definition of collaboration is "to work jointly with others or together, especially in an intellectual endeavor."

My plea is for a healthier relationship between actors and directors that will empower both and enhance the artistry. I am not suggesting that the director give up his or her vision. I am suggesting that the vision may alter or be made more complex when actors are brought on board as creators. As a director, there have been many times when I realized that the actor knows more about himself (his character) than I do despite my detailed preparation and study. I have been in casting rooms where an actor has been so true and committed that she changed my concept radically. I have also been in a position where I discovered, almost at the last rehearsal, that I had missed a vital structural point and therefore needed to go back and reframe certain scenes. Once I was able to release my own ego and admit that the actor standing in front of me arguing his point of view was right, I was excited to move ahead, and, indeed, fixing the problem did not turn out to be all that difficult.

The other piece of advice that I have to offer is that working with Superscenes and myth may at first appear to be a longer process than reading and blocking and running. However, I challenge you to try at least one scene in the Superscene way and one in the traditional way and see which you prefer. The advantages of Superscenes are that they go deeper and faster than the traditional method of rehearsal, they give the actors far more power, they reveal more complexities of relationship, and they are a tremendous aid to memory.

However you use the Superscenes and the other exercises in this book, feel free to experiment and let me know how they worked out. The only codicil is that if you are working using character language, very little may be accomplished. I had to train myself to use the language of action exclusively when talking to actors and to eliminate heady discussions of "who this guy is" and psychological analysis of the role. It took me a while, and actors wanted to talk about "him" or "her," but I insisted on the use of "I," as Stanislavski suggests, and that can make all the difference.

Selected bibliography

Becker, Ernest. *The Denial of Death.* New York: Free Press, 1973.

Blair, Rhonda. *The Actor, Image and Action: Acting and Cognitive Neuroscience.* London: Routledge Press, 2008.

Bogart, Ann, and Tina Landau. *The Viewpoints Book: A Practical Guide to Viewpoints and Composition.* New York: Theatre Communications Group, Inc., 2005.

Campbell, Joseph. *The Hero with a Thousand Faces.* 2nd Ed. Bollingen Series XVII, Princeton, NJ: Princeton, University Press, 1968.

Campbell, Joseph, and Bill Moyers. *The Power of Myth.* New York: Doubleday, 1998.

Carnicke, Sharon. *Stanislavski in Focus.* London: Routledge Press, 2003.

Casasanto, Daniel, and Katinka Dijkstra. "Motor Action and Emotional Memory". *Cognition* volume 115 (2010), 179–185.

Chambers, Catherine. *African Myths and Legends.* Ignite Series, All About Myths, Chicago: Raintree Press, 2013.

Charon, Joel. *Symbolic Interactionism: An Interaction, an Interpretation, an Integration.* Boston: Pearson, 2004.

Clark, Ella, and Margot Edmonds. *Voices of the Winds: Native American Legends.* New York: Castle Books, 2003.

Coupe, Laurence. *Myth.* The New Critical Idiom Series, London: Routledge Press, 1997.

———. *Kenneth Burke On Myth: An Introduction.* London: Routledge Press 2005.

Csikszentmihalyi, Mihaly. *Flow: The Psychology of Optimal Experience.* New York: Harper Perennial, Harper Collins Publishers, 1990.

Damasio, Antonio. *The Feeling of What Happens: Body, Emotion and the Making of Consciousness.* London: Heinemann, 1999.

———. *Looking for Spinoza: Joy Sorrow, and the Feeling Brain.* New York: Harvest Book, Harcourt Press, 2003.

Donnellan, Declan. *The Actor and the Target.* London: Nick Hern Books, 2005.

Edelman, Gerald, and Giulio Tononi. *A Universe of Consciousness: How Matter Becomes Imagination*. New York: Basic Books, Perseus Group, 2000.

Edinger, Edward F. *Ego and Archetype: Individuation and the Religious Function of the Psyche*. Boston: Shambhala Press, 1992.

Eliade, Mircea. *Myth and Reality*. New York: Harper and Row, 1963.

Gazzaniga, Michael. *Human: The Science Behind What Makes Us Unique*. New York: Harper Collins, 2008.

Gillette, Douglas, and Robert Moore. *King, Warrior, Magician, Lover: Rediscovering the Archetypes of the Mature Masculine*. San Francisco: Harper, 1990.

Goodwyn, Erik D. *The Neurobiology of the Gods: How Brain Physiology Shapes the Recurrent Imagery of Myth and Dreams*. London: Routledge, 2012.

Gordon, Mel. *The Stanislavsky Technique: Russia: A Workbook for Actors*. New York: Applause Books, 1987.

Gray, Richard. *Archetypal Explorations: An Integrative Approach to Human Behavior*. London: Routledge Press, 1996.

Hauser, Thomas, and Muhammad Ali. *Muhammad Ali: His Life and Times*. New York: Touchstone Books, 1991.

Holtcamp, Mark. *Biology of the Archetype*. (Free online book.) Amazon Digital Services, 2012.

Iacoboni, Mario. *Mirroring People*. New York: Farrar, Straus & Giroux, 2008.

Jacoby, Mario. *The Longing for Paradise: Psychological Perspectives on an Archetype*. Trans. Myron B. Gubitz. Boston: Sigo Press, 1985.

Jung, Carl. *The Collected Works of C.G. Jung*. Trans. R.F.C. Hull. Bollingen Series XX. Princeton, NJ: Princeton University Press, 1960.

Kandel, Eric. *In Search of Memory: The Emergence of a New Science of Mind*. New York: W.W. Norton & Company, 2006.

Kilner, J.M., and R.N. Lemon. "What We Know Currently about Mirror Neurons." *Current Biology* volume 23 issue 23 (Dec 2013). R1057–R1062.

Lakoff, George, and Mark Johnson. *Metaphors We Live By*. Chicago: The University of Chicago Press, 1980.

LeDoux, Joseph. *The Synaptic Self: How Our Brains Become Who We Are*. London: Penguin Books, 2002.

Llinas, Rodolfo R. *I of the Vortex: From Neurons to Self*. A Bradford Book. Cambridge, MA: MIT Press, 2002.

Luria, A.R. *The Mind of a Mnemonist*. Trans. Lynn Solotaroff. Cambridge, MA: Harvard University Press, 1968.

Marowitz, Charles. *Directing the Action: Acting and Directing in the Contemporary Theatre*. New York: Applause Theatre Books, 1986.

McKee, Robert. *Story: Substance, Structure, Style, and Principles of Screenwriting*. New York: Regan Books, 1997.

Modell, Arnold H. *Imagination and the Meaningful Brain*. A Bradford Book. Cambridge, MA: The MIT Press, 2006.

Murdock, Maureen. *The Heroine's Journey*. Boston: Shambhala Publishing, 1990.

Neumann, Erich. *The Origins and History of Consciousness*. 3rd Printing. Forward by C.G. Jung. Trans. R.F.C. Hull. Bollingen Series XLII, Princeton NJ: Princeton University Press, 1973.

Pinch, Geraldine. *Egyptian Mythology: A Guide to the Gods and Goddesses of Egypt*. Oxford, England: Oxford Press, 2002.

Ramachandran, V.S., and Sandra Blakeslee. *Phantoms in the Brain: Probing the Mysteries of the Human Mind*. New York: Harper Perennial Books, 1998.

Rauch, Stephen. *Neil Gaiman's The Sandman: In Search of the Modern Myth*. Pennsylvania: Wildside Press, April, 2003.

Richards, Thomas. *At Work With Grotowski on Physical Actions*. London: Routledge, 1993.

Roach, Joseph. *The Player's Passion: Studies in the Science of Acting*. Ann Arbor: University of Michigan Press, 2002.

Schechner, Richard. *Between Theatre and Anthropology*. Philadelphia: University of Pennsylvania Press, 1985.

Shlain, Leonard. *The Alphabet Versus the Goddess: The Conflict Between Word and Image*. New York: Viking Press, 1998.

Stanislavski, Konstantin. *An Actor's Work: A Student's Diary*. Trans. Jean Benedetti. London: Routledge Press, 2008.

Stephens, Anthony. *The Two Million Year Old Self*. Carolyn and Ernest Fay Series in Analytical Psychology (Book 3). College Station, TX: A&M University Press, 2005.

Temkine, Raymonde. *Grotowski*. Trans. Alex Szogyi. New York: Avon Books, 1972.

Thompson, Evan. *Mind in Life: Biology, Phenomenology, and the Sciences of the Mind*. Cambridge, MA: Cambridge Press, 2007.

Turner, Victor. *From Ritual to Theatre: The Human Seriousness of Play*. New York: Performing Arts Journal Press, 1982.

———. *The Ritual Process: Structure and Anti-Structure*. Second Printing of 1969 original edition. New Brunswick, NJ: Aldine Transaction Publishers, 2009.

Varela, Francisco, Evan Thompson, and Eleanor Rosch. *The Embodied Mind: Cognitive Science and Human Experience*. Cambridge, MA: The MIT Press, 1993.

Williams, David. *The Trickster Brain: Neuroscience, Evolution, and Nature*. Lanham, MD: Lexington Books, February 27, 2013.

Index